OKLAHOMA

C O O K   B O O K

Edited by
Mary Beth Lilley

**GOLDEN
WEST** ☼
PUBLISHERS

Printed in the United States of America
4th Printing © 2007

ISBN13: 978-1-885590-49-7
ISBN10: 1-885590-49-0

Golden West Publishers
4113 N. Longview Ave.
Phoenix, AZ 85014, USA
(602)265-4392
(800)658-5830

For free sample recipes for every Golden West cookbook, visit:
www.goldenwestpublishers.com

TABLE OF CONTENTS

SIDE DISHES

BREADS

DESSERTS

ABOUT THE EDITOR

WELCOME TO OKLAHOMA!

From the Indian Fry Bread to Chicken Fried Steak this cookbook presents home grown recipes that encompass ethnic traditions from Native Americans to Polish immigrants as well as the Mennonites who settled in what was Indian Territory. So bent on being farmers were the Mennonites that women sewed Turkey Red wheat (a hard red winter variety used for breads) into the hems of their dresses and carried it to their new homes in a hostile land.

Oklahoma is a proud land. It is home to the largest number of Native American tribes. Famous Indians—including Black Kettle, Roman Nose, Geronimo and Sequoyah—have left their moccasin tracks in Oklahoma's red earth.

Oklahoma is a fertile land. Its rivers, creeks and lakes are home to dozens of species of fish and wildlife. It is a diverse state, resplendent in beautiful mountains, waterfalls, canyons and plains. Oklahoma farmers are the producers of the second largest winter wheat and rye harvests in America.

Breads of course are featured on nearly every table in the state. It is home to three major flour mills. Oklahoma ranks fourth in the nation in the production of hay, pecans and cattle; fifth in grain sorghum; seventh in peanuts; eighth in hogs; 10th in watermelons and 12th in broilers sold. Oklahoma has 33.2 million acres of land in farms in its 69,919 square miles. Many Oklahoma homesteaders relied on 'taters and beans to get them through lean years.

Enjoy these recipes as you learn the history and the unique down-home taste of Oklahoma cooking!

The name Oklahoma is a combination of two Choctaw Indian words—**okla**, meaning people, and **homma**, meaning red.

Some notable Oklahomans: **Athletes:** Jim Thorpe, Troy Aikman, Mickey Mantle **Actors/Actresses:** Lon Chaney & Lon Chaney Jr., Joan Crawford, James Garner, Alice Ghostly, Donna Reed, Chuck Norris, Brad Pitt, Ron Howard, Tom Mix, William "Hopalong" Cassidy, Will Rogers, **Musicians/Singers:** Garth Brooks, John Denver, Vince Gill, Roger Miller, Reba McEntire, Patti Page, Conway Twitty, **Astronaut:** Gordon Cooper Broadcast Journalists: Hugo & Walter Cronkite, Paul Harvey.

For information about Oklahoma: http://www.oklaosf.state.ok.us

OKLAHOMA FACTS

SIZE	69,919 sq. mi.
STATEHOOD	Nov. 16, 1907–46th state
MUSICAL INSTRUMENT	Fiddle
NICKNAME	The Sooner/Boomer State
CAPITAL	Oklahoma City
MOTTO	Labor Conquers All Things
HIGHEST ELEVATION	Black Mesa, 4,973 ft.
TREE	Redbud
SONG	Oklahoma!
ANIMAL	American Buffalo
BIRD	Scissor Tailed Flycatcher
FLOWER	Mistletoe
FISH	White Bass
COLORS	Green and White
REPTILE	Collared Lizard
WILDFLOWER	Indian Blanket

APPETIZERS & BEVERAGES

Recipe: _____

From: _____

Ingredients: _____ _____

_____ _____

_____ _____

_____ _____

_____ _____

_____ _____

Directions: _____

_____

_____

_____

_____

_____

Recipe: _____

From: _____

Ingredients: _____ _____

_____ _____

_____ _____

_____ _____

_____ _____

_____ _____

Directions: _____

_____

_____

_____

_____

_____

QUICK & EASY APPETIZER
"This is a great solution when you need a quick, last-minute dish."
Sara Fleming-Covington

1 pkg.(8-inch) **Flour Tortillas**
1 pkg.(4oz.) **Cream Cheese**, softened
1 tbsp. chopped **Chives** (freeze-dried or fresh)
Thin Sliced **Deli Meat** of your choice

Spread flour tortillas with cream cheese. Sprinkle with chives. Add a layer of deli meat. Roll flour tortilla up firmly. Slice into 1-inch thick pieces. Turn slices onto their sides with the swirl showing and place on a serving plate.
Serves 8-10 if package of 12 tortillas is used.

SPINACH—PARSLEY HORS D' OEUVRES
"This is a sparkly addition to any snack table or buffet."
Mary Frances Myers-Tulsa

1 pkg.(10.75oz.) frozen **Spinach,** chopped
2 cups chopped **Fresh Parsley**
1/2 tsp. **Salt**
1 tsp. **Black Pepper**
Mayonnaise

Thaw spinach and squeeze out water. Mix with remaining ingredients using just enough mayonnaise to hold mixture together. Serve with crackers.
Enough for 80-100 crackers

Tulsa
Tulsa is home to the Gilcrease Museum, which houses the world's largest collection of art of the American West. One of its landmarks is Oral Roberts University with its 200-foot prayer tower. The name Tulsa is derived from the Creek word "Tullahassee" meaning "old town."

DAFFODIL VEGGIE DIP
"This is the best vegetable dip I have ever eaten".
Patsy Warman–Dewey

2 pkgs.(8oz.ea.) **Cream Cheese**
2 tbsp. **Mayonnaise**
4 hard–boiled **Eggs**, mashed
1 tsp **Garlic Powder**
1 tsp **Salt**
1 cup fresh **Parsley**

Combine all ingredients; mix well. Refrigerate
at least one hour before serving.
Serves 6–8.

JAN'S SALSA
"This recipe is actually a combination of two recipes given to me by my
daughter–in–law and one of my sons."
Jan Susan Wood–Aunt Jan's Cozy Cottage Bed & Breakfast, Spiro

5 lg. **Jalapenos**
4 cans (1 lb. ea.) **Stewed Tomatoes** (drain juice and reserve)
5 lg. fresh cloves **Garlic**, peeled
1 bunch **Cilantro**, stems removed
1 bunch **Green Onions**, chopped
1 lg. **Tomato**, chopped

Remove tops from jalapenos and remove the seeds from 3 to 4 of them
depending on your desire for "heat." Put tomato juice in blender. Add jalapeños,
garlic, and cilantro and blend. Pour half of mixture into a large bowl. Add stewed
tomatoes to remaining mixture in blender and chop about 5 seconds. Do not
purée. Add this to mixture in bowl. Add green onions and fresh tomato. Serve
with chips.

Makes 2 1/2 quarts salsa.

MEXICAN MINI—PIZZAS
"This is a favorite appetizer in our house."
Karen Barnes—Ames

1 can (16oz.) **Refried Beans**
6 (8-inch) **Flour Tortillas**
10 oz. **Monterey Jack Cheese** grated
Salsa, fresh or canned

Spread refried beans evenly over flour tortillas and sprinkle with cheese. Place on cookie sheets and bake in a 400 degree oven for about 10 minutes or until cheese is melted. Top with salsa to taste. Cut each into six pieces and serve. Serves 4.

MOREY'S SALSA
"I love to cook, and make a mean salsa served as a dip or to garnish Mexican food. I plan to become a professional chef."
Morey Hutchison—Canton

5-6 **Roma Tomatoes** chopped
1 **Sweet Red** or **White Onion** chopped
1 **Green Bell Pepper** chopped
1 can (2.5oz.) **Black Olives,** drained and chopped
1 **Avocado,** peeled and diced
Juice of 1 **Lemon**
2-3 tbsp. **Vinegar** (to taste)
2-3 tbsp. **Olive Oil** (to taste)
Sprig of fresh **Cilantro**
Salt and **Pepper** to taste

Mix ingredients, chill for several hours before serving. Recipe may be doubled or tripled. Serves 6-8.

For spicier salsa, add 1 **Jalapeno Pepper,** chopped, or 1 can (4oz.) diced **Green Chiles.**

ROAD KILL

"This has been a staple for years but no one ever seemed to have a name for it, so some men at a party decided to call it Road Kill and that's been its name ever since. We never confuse it with anything else."
Karen Barnes–Ames

1 can (4.5oz.) **Olives**, chopped
1 pkg. (8oz.) **Cream Cheese**, softened
1 jar (2.25oz.) **Dried Beef,** diced
Green Onions, chopped

Drain liquid from olives and combine with all other ingredients. Keep refrigerated until serving time. Spread on crackers.
Serves 4

SHRIMP DIP

"This is an extra–special dish I use for Christmas and other special events."
Mona Lee Brock–Madill

1 pkg. unflavored **Gelatin**
1/4 cup **Warm Water**
3 pkgs. (8oz.ea.) **Cream Cheese,** softened
1/2 cup **Mayonnaise**
1 can (10.75 oz.)**Tomato Soup**
1/2 cup diced **Onion**
1/2 cup diced **Celery**
1/2 cup diced **Green Bell Pepper**
2 cans (4.25 oz. ea.) **Tiny Shrimp,** drained

Dissolve gelatin in warm water. Beat cream cheese slowly with mixer. Add the mayonnaise, gelatin and tomato soup. Beat with mixer until fluffy. Add the rest of the ingredients and mix well with a spoon. Refrigerate overnight for best flavor. Serve with crackers.
Serves 8–12.

Oklahoma City

Oklahoma's capital city was established in 1910 and is the only capital in the world surrounded by working oil wells. There's also an operational well <u>beneath</u> the city! Among the city's offerings are the largest National Guard Museum in the U.S., the National Cowboy Hall of Fame and Western Heritage Center, and the National Softball Hall of Fame and Museum. Stockyards City, in the southwestern part of the city, was founded in 1910 and is still the largest stocker/feeder cattle market in the world.

BANANA PUNCH
"I have served this for years at Democratic teas in my home and it always gets praise." Sweet Pea Abernathy—Altus

4 cups **Sugar**
6 cups **Water**
1 can (46oz.) **Pineapple Juice**
1 can (12oz.) frozen **Orange Juice,** thawed

1 qt. **Water**
6 **Bananas**
2 qts. **Ginger Ale**

Combine sugar and 6 cups water in a saucepan, bring to a boil and boil for 5 minutes. Combine juices with 1 quart water. Blend bananas in blender with a little of the boiled sugar and water mixture. Combine all ingredients (except ginger ale) thoroughly and freeze. Thaw 2–3 hour before serving. Add chilled ginger ale to punch when ready to serve. Serves 18–20.

WEDDING FRUIT PUNCH
"I received this recipe from my mother."
Mary Whitehead—Billings

10 lg **Oranges**, juiced
10 lg. **Lemons**, juiced
4 qts. fresh **Strawberrie**s (if frozen, thaw), crushed
2 liters **Ginger Ale**
2 liters **7–up**

Mix juices with strawberries. Chill overnight. When ready to serve, stir in chilled ginger ale and 7–Up. Serve with crushed ice. Serves 50.

Recipe: _____

From: _____

Ingredients: _____ _____

_____ _____

_____ _____

_____ _____

_____ _____

_____ _____

Directions: _____

_____

_____

_____

_____

_____

Recipe: _____

From: _____

Ingredients: _____ _____

_____ _____

_____ _____

_____ _____

_____ _____

_____ _____

Directions: _____

_____

_____

_____

_____

_____

BREAKFAST & BRUNCH

Panhandle Pancakes
Farmer's & Rancher's Breakfast
Breakfast Wheat
Nectarine Fritters with Orange Blossom Syrup
Impossible Quiche
Fried Mush
German Egg Pancakes
Breakfast Casserole
Crouton Breakfast Casserole
Social Scrambled Eggs
DG's Spectacular French Toast
Broiled Grapefruit
Sourdough Pancakes
Crab Quiche

PANHANDLE PANCAKES
"My guests enjoy these and I serve them often."
Virginia Strong—Virginia's Bed and Breakfast, Boise City

4 cups sifted **Flour**
2 tbsp. **Baking Powder**
1 1/2 tsp. **Salt**
2 tbsp. **Sugar**
4 **Eggs,** separated
3 cups **Milk***
3/4 cup melted **Butter**

Sift together the flour, baking powder, salt and sugar. In another bowl beat egg yolks, milk and butter. Add to flour mixture, mixing only until flour is moistened. Beat eggs whites and fold into mixture. Fry pancakes on hot griddle. Can store in covered pitcher in refrigerator for several days.
Makes about 16 medium—size pancakes.

*Use only 2 1/2 cups milk if making waffles.

BREAKFAST WHEAT
"This can also be used in meatloaves and salad toppings."
Norma Kirby—Lamont

1 qt. **Wheat Berries** (kernels)
Water to cover

Thrash (clean) wheat several times. Put cleaned wheat in water to just cover. Boil over low/medium heat 2–3 hours or until soft. Watch that mixture doesn't dry out. Stir occasionally. As wheat becomes cooked and soft the water is absorbed. Refrigerate. Serve as a s breakfast cereal with cream and sugar. Serves 8–12.

FARMER'S & RANCHER'S BREAKFAST

"My husband, Newley, and I oversee the Chain Ranch's hunting and fishing leases and entertain lots of sportsmen. I often serve this hearty breakfast dish and everyone loves it."
Mandy Hutchison—Chain Ranch, Canton

2 lbs. **Bacon**
1 lg. **Onion,** chopped
1 lg. **Green Bell Pepper,** diced
6 cups cubed raw **Potatoes**
Salt and **Pepper** to taste
12 **Eggs,** beaten
1 cup **Milk**
1 tsp **Pimento**
1 tsp **Tabasco® Sauce**
1 lb. grated **Cheese**

Cut bacon into small pieces, place in a Dutch oven and cook until lightly browned. Add onion and pepper: cook until tender. Remove from Dutch oven, Drain all but a small amount of bacon drippings from oven: add cubed potatoes and fry until soft. Add the cooked bacon, onion and pepper. Season lightly with salt and pepper and mix well. Break eggs into a mixing bowl and beat thoroughly. Combine eggs with milk, pimento and Tabasco sauce; pour over potatoes. Cover Dutch oven. When eggs are nearly set, sprinkle grated cheese on mixture, replace lid and cook until cheese melts.
Serves 8–12.

NECTARINE FRITTERS WITH ORANGE BLOSSOM SYRUP

"This recipe is a very special treat to our guests. Everyone comments on how beautiful this breakfast looks."
Earl Plummer—This Plum Tree Bed and Breakfast, Salina

1 cup **Flour**
1 tsp. **Baking Powder**
1 tsp. **Salt**
2 **Eggs**
3 cups fresh unpared, sliced **Nectarines**

1/2 cup **Half and Half**
1 tsp. **Vegetable Oil**
Powdered Sugar
Nutmeg

Combine flour, baking powder, salt, eggs half and half and vegetable oil. Beat until batter is smooth. Fold in nectarines. Heat a small amount of vegetable oil in a 10-inch skillet at 375 degrees. Drop batter from a tablespoon into oil, turning once to brown both sides. Remove with slotted spoon and drain on paper towels. Sprinkle with powdered sugar and nutmeg while warm. Serve with **Orange Blossom Syrup**.
Serves 2-4.

ORANGE BLOSSOM SYRUP

1 tsp **Orange Extract**
1/2 cup **Pancake Syrup**

Mix extract with syrup and warm in microwave. Double or triple recipe as needed.

Did You Know?
There are more Native American tribes and the highest population of Indians in Oklahoma than any other state.

IMPOSSIBLE QUICHE
"This recipe was give to me by my oldest daughter",
Jill Susan Wood Garcia."
Jan Wood—Aunt Jan's Cozy Cottage B & B, Spiro

Cheddar or **Mozzarella Cheese** (or a combination), grated
Sausage and **Ham,** chopped
Green Bell Peppers, chopped
1 fresh **Tomato**, chopped
Broccoli or **Spinach,** chopped
4 **Eggs**
1/2 cup **Bisquick®**
2 cups **Milk**
Salt and **Pepper** to taste

Spread desired amounts of cheese, meat and vegetables in a 9-inch lightly greased pie pan. Combine remaining ingredients in blender for 1 minute: pour over top of mixture in pie pan. Bake for 50-55 minutes at 350 degrees or until tests done. Serves 6.

FRIED MUSH
"My parents were farmers. Mother used to make this a regular part of our breakfast. Serve it with homegrown honey or maple syrup. My father loved it with molasses."
Mary Beth Lilley—Enid

4 cups **Water**, divided   1 1/2 tsp. **Salt**   1 cup **Cornmeal**

Bring 3 cups of water and the salt to a boil. Gradually add a mixture of 1 cup cornmeal and 1 cup cold water, stirring constantly until mixture is thickened. Cover, lower heat and cook slowly 10 minutes or longer. Pour hot mush into a well-oiled or buttered loaf pan. When cooled, cover and chill thoroughly. Remove from pan, cut into slices 1/2 to 1 inch thick, depending on taste. Dip into flour or cornmeal and fry on both sides on a well-buttered or oiled hot griddle until browned. Serves 6-8.

GERMAN EGG PANCAKES
Linda Byrd–The Byrd House Bed and Breakfast, Guthrie

4 tbsp. **Butter**
8 large **Eggs**
2/3 cup **Milk**
2/3 cup **All–Purpose Flour** or **Cake Flour**
1/2 tsp **Salt**

1 tart **Apple**, peeled and
   sliced paper thin
1 tbsp. **Vanilla**
Lemon or **Lime Juice**
Powdered Sugar

Preheat oven to 350 degrees. Place butter in an ovenproof round dish. An iron skillet works great. Heat the butter until it is melted and bubbly. Beat eggs for 1 minute, add milk, flour, salt and vanilla. Mix together. Rotate baking dish from side to side to coat the interior with the butter. Pour egg mixture into dish and place apples on top. Cook for 25–30 minutes. The edges of the pancake will ruffle up and the center become fairly firm. Cut into generous wedges and serve with fresh lemon or lime juice to be squeezed on top. Sprinkle with powdered sugar.
Serves 4.

BREAKFAST CASSEROLE
"This is really good. Any kind of cheese can be used."
Rosailla Fuksa–Bison

6 **Eggs**, beaten
2 cups **Milk**
1 tsp. **Salt**
1 tsp. dry **Mustard**
3 slices **Bread**, cubed
1 lb. cooked **Sausage**
1 cup shredded **Cheese**

In a bowl, beat together eggs, milk, salt and mustard. Grease a 9 x 13 baking pan. Layer bread, sausage and then cheese. Pour beaten egg mixture over top. Bake in a 350 degree oven for 45 minutes.
Serves 4.

CROUTON BREAKFAST CASSEROLE
**"This casserole can be made quickly and is a favorite
with many of our guests."**
**David & Kami Ratcliff–Campbell–Richison House Bed & Breakfast,
Chickasha**

1 cup **Herb–Seasoned Croutons**
1 cup cooked **Sausage** or 4 slices **Bacon** or 4 oz. shaved **Ham**
1/2 cup **Cheddar Cheese**
4 **Eggs**, beaten

Preheat oven to 350 degrees. Spray 2 individual casserole dishes (about the size of miniature pie tins)* with nonstick cooking spray. Sprinkle the croutons in the bottom of the dishes. Follow with half of the meat you have chosen to use. Sprinkle half of the cheese over the top of each. Pour beaten eggs over both dishes and place in oven immediately. Bake for 20–25 minutes or until eggs are set.
Serves 2.

* If you do not have individual casseroles, use an 8 x 8 square cake pan and layer all ingredients in order given.

SPECIAL SCRAMBLED EGGS
"The sour cream makes this dish special."
Jennifer & Brent Kisling–Maple Place Bed & Breakfast, Enid

3 **Eggs**
1 tbsp. **Sour Cream**
Cheddar Cheese, finely shredded

Whisk together sour cream and eggs. Scramble as usual. After taking eggs from skillet, top with cheese. Allow to melt evenly over eggs.
Serves 1–2.

DG'S SPECTACULAR FRENCH TOAST
"This is a delight for the eyes as well as satisfying to that sweet tooth!"
Cindy and Gary Worthington–Worthington House Bed & Breakfast, Enid

2 **Eggs**
3 oz. **Milk**
2 tbsp. **Cream**
1/2 tsp. **Vanilla**
Pinch **Nutmeg**
French Bread, cut in 1–ich slices
Crushed **Corn Flakes**

Make dipping batter for French toast by combining eggs, milk, cream, vanilla and nutmeg. Dip bread slices in batter on both sides, then dredge one side in crushed cornflakes. Fry on heated griddle until golden brown. Place hot French toast (3 pieces per serving) on warmed plate. Top with the following in order given: warmed Maple Syrup, 3 small scoops Vanilla Ice Cream, warmed Caramel Topping, Mini Chocolate Chips ,several dollops Whipped Cream, and sprinkle of chopped Nuts. Garnish with a Maraschino Cherry.
Serves 4–6

BROILED GRAPEFRUIT
"This is a favorite breakfast dish at my 1905
Dutch Victorian Bed & Breakfast."
Linda L. Byrd–The Byrd House Bed & Breakfast, Guthrie

Cut **Grapefruit** in half and cut membrane sections
Sprinkle 1 tbsp. **Brown Sugar** on top of each half
Place 1 pat of **Butter** in the center of each half
Place grapefruit halves in an ovenproof baking dish. Cook under broiler 10–15 minutes at 325 degrees.
Serves 2.

SOURDOUGH PANCAKES
Norma Kirby–Lamont

2 cups **Flour**
2 cups **Warm Water**
1/2 cup **Sourdough Starter** (pg 66)
2 tbsp. **Sugar**
1/2 tsp. **Salt**

1/2 tsp. **Baking Powder**
3 tbsp. **Cooking Oil**
2 **Eggs,** slightly beaten
1/2 tsp. **Baking Soda**
1 tbsp. **Water**

Mix flour, 2 cups warm water and sourdough starter; beat with wooden spoon until smooth. Cover. Let stand in a warm place overnight. Add sugar, salt, baking powder, oil and eggs to the batter; beat well. Batter will be lumpy. Dissolve baking soda in 1 tablespoon water and stir into batter. Bake on greased griddle. Serves 6–8.

CRAB QUICHE
**"This is excellent served as a breakfast entrée.
We also serve it often at our afternoon teas."**
Cindy and Gary Worthington–Worthington House Bed & Breakfast, Enid

3 **Eggs,** beaten
1 cup **Sour Cream**
1/2 tsp. **Worcestershire Sauce**
3/4 tsp. **Salt**
1 cup shredded **Swiss Cheese**
1 can (7 oz.) **Crabmeat**, drained and flaked
1 can (3 oz.) **French Fried Onions**
2 (9–inch) baked **Pastry Shells**

Preheat oven to 300 degrees. Combine eggs, sour cream, Worcestershire sauce and salt. Stir in cheese, crabmeat and fried onions. Pour into pastry shells. Bake 1 hour or until set. Serve hot in small wedges.
Serves 12–16.

Recipe: _____
From: _____
Ingredients: _____ _____
_____ _____
_____ _____
_____ _____
_____ _____

Directions: _____
_____
_____
_____
_____
_____

Recipe: _____
From: _____
Ingredients: _____ _____
_____ _____
_____ _____
_____ _____
_____ _____

Directions: _____
_____
_____
_____
_____
_____

Soups, Stews & Salads

MEXICAN SOUP OKLAHOMA—STYLE
"Our guests enjoy this easy and delicious soup."
Mandy Hutchison–Chain Ranch, Canton

2 tbsp. minced **Garlic**
2 tbsp. **Butter**
2 tbsp. ground **Cumin**
2 cans (14 oz. ea.) **Chicken Broth**
2 cans (14 oz. ea.) **Stewed Tomatoes**, undrained
1 cup **Picante Sauce**
1/2 cup chopped **Celery**
4 1/2 cups cooked and shredded **Chicken**
2 cans (15oz. ea.) **Corn**
1 can (4 oz.) diced **Green Chiles**
1/2 cup chopped **Cilantro**

In a skillet, sauté garlic in butter, add cumin; cook and stir 1 minute. Add broth, tomatoes, picante sauce, celery, chicken, corn, chiles and cilantro. Bring to boil. Reduce heat: cover and simmer for 30 minutes. Pour hot soup over **Tortilla Strips** in serving bowls and top with grated **Monterey Jack Cheese**, or serve with warm, buttered and rolled Tortillas on the side.
Serves 4–6

PEACHES' BRUNSWICK STEW

"When we moved to Enid from Georgia, we found that Brunswick Stew was often found in Oklahoma kitchens. We decided to create our own version of this favorite dish." John and Lisa Dixon—Enid

1 whole (4–5 lb) **Chicken**
2 cups canned or frozen **Lima Beans**
1 cup canned or frozen **Whole Kernel Corn**
1 can (15 oz.) **Cream Style Corn**
1 cup chopped **Onions**
2 cans (14.5 oz. ea) **Stewed Tomatoes**
1 cup minced **Green Bell Pepper**
2 cups **Ketchup**
1/2 cup **Mustard**
1/3 cup **Worcestershire Sauce**
1 cup **Dill Pickle Juice**
1/2 cup **Sugar**
2 tsp. **Black Pepper**
2 tbsp. **Garlic Powder**
2 tsp. **Salt**
2 tbsp. **Paprika**
2 tbsp. **Lemon Juice**
Hot Sauce, to taste

In a large saucepan, boil whole chicken until it separates from the bone. Remove chicken from saucepan, reserving 1 cup broth and debone. Combine all other ingredients in a large stockpot* and bring to a hard boil for 5 minutes. Reduce heat, cover and simmer with cover tilted to release steam until vegetables are done. Add deboned chicken and 1 cup broth to stock pot and continue to simmer for about 1 hour. Remove from heat and use a utensil, such as a potato masher, to mash all ingredients. Return to heat, recover pot with lid tilted and simmer 1.5 to 2 hours.
*A crockpot works well for this recipe.
Serves 6–8.

HAMBURGER STEW

"This recipe was given to me by a childhood friend, Virginia Smith, some 40 years ago. My family never tires of it and drop in company raves about how delicious it is."
Mona Lee Brock—Madill

1 lb. lean **Ground Beef**
1 chopped **Onion**
1 can (8oz.) **Tomato Sauce**
1 can (8oz.) **Tomato Paste**
3 cups **Water**
Salt to taste
1 tsp. each: **Accent®, Chili Powder, Oregano** and **Cumin**
1 tbsp. **Sugar**
2 cloves **Garlic,** crushed
1 cup cooked **Rice**

Brown beef with chopped onion. Add tomato sauce, tomato paste and three cups of water. Add salt, Accent®, chili powder, oregano, cumin, sugar, and garlic. Simmer slowly about 35 minutes. Add cooked rice. Serve in individual serving dishes with bowls of grated **Cheese**, shredded **Lettuce**, chopped **Olives**, chopped **Tomatoes**, **Green Onions** and **Corn Chips** on the side.
Serves 4.

Lake Texoma

Just 15 miles east of Madill is beautiful Lake Texoma, one of the largest man-made lakes in the United States. It covers 140 square miles on the Texas and Oklahoma border. The lake was formed in 1944 by Denison Dam, which was built on the Red River to produce hydroelectric power, control floods and allow navigation. Lake Texoma has become popular for fishing, hunting and water sports.

WILTED LETTUCE SALAD
"This was a summer treat my mother made while I was growing up on the family farm." Jane Spreier–Okeene

4 slices **Bacon**
1/4 cup **Vinegar**
3 tbsp. **Sugar**
Salt and **Pepper** to taste
1/4 cup chopped **Green Onions** with tops
Lettuce

In a skillet, fry bacon until crisp; remove bacon to paper towels. Combine remaining ingredients (except lettuce) in bacon drippings and bring to a boil. Sprinkle vinegar mixture over lettuce; toss. Crumble bacon over the top and serve. Serves 2.

CHAIN RANCH CHILI
"We got this recipe more than 20 years ago at a church gathering and have enjoyed it ever since." Andre Hutchinson–Chain Ranch, Canton

1 1/2 to 2 lbs. **Ground Beef**
1 tbsp. **Garlic Powder**
1 can (48 oz.) **Tomato Juice**
1 tbsp. **Chili Powder**
1 tbsp. **Cumin**
Salt and **Pepper** to taste

In a large skillet, brown beef and drain. Add remaining ingredients and cook for several hours until thick.

Serving suggestions: Serve this chili on a plate of crushed **Tortilla Chips** with the following ingredients layered on top: **Brown Rice, Lettuce**, chopped **Tomatoes, Onions, Green Bell Peppers, Black Olives, Mushrooms, Nuts, Coconut, Pineapple Tidbits, Sour Cream** and **Picante Sauce**.
Serves 6–8.

RAW CRANBERRY SALAD
"This is my favorite dish to take to Christmas dinners."
Minnie Mendell–Talala

1 pkg. (12oz.) **Cranberries**
3 cups **Sugar**
1 pkg. (6 oz.) **Cherry Jell–o®**
1 can (8oz.) crushed **Pineapple**
2 cups finely chopped **Apples**
2 **Oranges,** cut up
2 cups whole or chopped **Pecans**
1 1/2 cups **Mini–Marshmallows**

Grind cranberries, sprinkle with sugar and let set 2 hours. Make Jell–o, using the amount of hot water mentioned on box, but do not add cold water. Add cranberries and remaining ingredients to gelatin mixture; refrigerate. Can be made a day or two ahead.
Serves 4–6.

GRANDMOTHERS GRACE'S HAMBURGER SLAW
"This tangy slaw is served whenever we barbecue hamburgers."
Andrea Hutchinson–Canton

1/2 head **Cabbage,** chopped
1/2 cup chopped **Dill Pickles**
1/2 cup chopped **Onions**
1/4 cup prepared **Mustard**
1/4 to 1/2 cup **Miracle Whip®** or **Mayonnaise**
Salt and **Pepper** to taste

Mix all ingredients well and refrigerate until ready to serve.
Serves 4.

PAT'S SALAD
"The dressing makes this a great salad!"
Kate Morrison–Enid

1 lg. head **Romaine** or green leaf **Lettuce**
1 pkg. slivered **Almonds**, toasted
1 can (15oz.) **Pineapple Tidbits,** drained
6–8 **Green Onions,** sliced thin

Toss lettuce, almonds, pineapple and onions together in a large bowl. Pour **Poppy Seed Dressing** over all and toss again.
Serves 6–8.

POPPY SEED DRESSING

2–3 tsp. **Poppy Seeds**   2 tbsp. **White Rice Vinegar**
1/2 tsp. **Dry Mustard**   1/2 tsp. **Salt**
1/2 cup **Salad Oil**   1/4 cup **Sugar**
Juice of 1/2 **Lemon**

Combine all ingredients and pour over salad.

ROSAILLA'S SALAD
"I learned to make this in the 1940s when I first learned to cook."
Rosailla Fuksa–Bison

2 tbsp. **Butter**   2 tbsp. **Water**
2 **Eggs**   1 pkg. **Marshmallows** cut up or 1 pkg. **Mini–Marshmallows**
4 tbsp. **Vinegar**   1 cup crushed **Pineapple**
2 tbsp. **Mustard**   1 cup **Nuts**
1 tbsp. **Sugar**   1 cup **Whipped Cream**

Cook butter, eggs, vinegar, mustard, sugar and water in saucepan: then add the marshmallows, crushed pineapple and nuts. Mix well. Chill overnight. Before serving, blend in whipped cream. Serves 4–6.

OKLAHOMA SLAW

"This is better if refrigerated for several days. It keeps well."
Ivon Choate–Waukomis

1 lg. head **Cabbage**
1 lg. **Onion**
1 med. **Green Bell Pepper**
1 med. **Red Bell Pepper**
1 1/2 cups **Sugar**

1 cup **Vinegar**
3/4 cup **Wesson® Oil**
1 1/2 tbsp. **Dry Mustard**
1 tsp. **Celery Seed**

Shred cabbage. Cut onion and peppers into small pieces. Place vegetables in a large bowl and sprinkle with sugar. In a saucepan, heat the vinegar, oil, dry mustard and celery seed to a rolling boil. Pour over vegetables. Stir and chill for at least hour hours.
Serves 6–8.

LIME SALAD

"I came across this recipe many years ago and it was love at first bite. It's a great dish for church suppers and family get–togethers."
Kathie Stocksen–Enid

1 pkg. (6oz.) **Lime Gelatin**
2 cups **Hot Water**
2 tbsp. grated **Onion**
1 can (15 1/2 oz.) crushed **Pineapple**, undrained
2 cups small curd **Cottage Cheese**
1 cup **Mayonnaise**

Dissolve gelatin in hot water and chill until syrupy. With a rotary beater or hand mixer, beat until fluffy. Add onion, pineapple and cottage cheese; mix well. Add mayonnaise and blend until smooth. Pour into a 9 x 13 pan and refrigerate until firm. Cut into squares to serve.
Serves 8–10.

PINK ARTIC FREEZE

"My mother started making this dish when I was a young girl. Our family always looks for it on the Thanksgiving Table each year."
Kate Morrison–Enid

1 pkg. (8oz.) **Cream Cheese,** softened
2 tbsp. **Mayonnaise**
2 tbsp. **Sugar**
1 1/3 cup whole **Cranberry Sauce**
1 can (9oz.) crushed **Pineapple**, drained
1/2 cup chopped **Walnuts**
1 cup **Whipped Topping**

Mix together the cream cheese, mayonnaise and sugar until well blended. Stir in fruit and nuts then fold in whipped topping. Pour into a loaf pan and freeze until firm. Before serving, let stand at room temperature 15 minutes, then slice and serve immediately.
Serve 8–10.

COOL WHIP SALAD

"I got this recipe from Evelyn Beagley. Her husband, Ot, worked in our rodeos."
Minnie and Willie Mendell–Mendell Rodeo Co., Talala

1 can (20 oz.) crushed **Pineapple**
1 cup **Sugar**
1 envelope **Knox® Gelatin**
1/4 cup **Cold Water**

8 oz. grated **American Cheese**
1 cup **Pecans**
1 sm. carton **Cool Whip®**

In a saucepan, bring pineapple and sugar to a boil; set aside to cool. Soften in cold water and then add to pineapple mixture. Mix the cheese, pecans and Cool Whip together; combine with pineapple mixture. Refrigerate for at least two hours before serving.
Serves 6–8.

Recipe: _____

From: _____

Ingredients: _____ _____

_____ _____

_____ _____

_____ _____

_____ _____

_____ _____

Directions: _____

_____

_____

_____

_____

_____

Recipe: _____

From: _____

Ingredients: _____ _____

_____ _____

_____ _____

_____ _____

_____ _____

_____ _____

Directions: _____

_____

_____

_____

_____

_____

Main Dishes

Chicken Fried Steak
Sunday Supper Meatloaf
Cowboy Fajitas
Ranch Stroganoff
Bierocks
Kathie's Chicken Fried Steak
Chicken Casserole
Goulash
Enchilada Casserole
Buffalo Summer Sausage

Baked Steak
Mexican Casserole
German Hot Sandwich
Firefighter Beans
Smoke Call Beans
Flashover Beans
False Alarm Beans
Backdraft Beans

Fried Tuna Patties
King Ranch Chicken
Hobo Suppers
Enchiladas
Ralph's Beer Meatloaf
Swedish Meatballs
Great Aunt Verda's Chicken Enchiladas

CHICKEN FRIED STEAK

This is the centerpiece of one of the official State of Oklahoma meals."
Mary Beth Lilley—Enid

1 **Egg,** slightly beaten
1/2 cup **Buttermilk**
1/2 cup **Water**
1 tsp. **Worcestershire Sauce**
2/3 cup **All—Purpose Flour**
1/2 tsp. **Salt**
1/2 tsp. **Black Pepper**
7 (4 oz. ea.) **Cube Steaks**
Vegetable Oil

Combine egg, buttermilk, water and Worcestershire sauce. Mix well. Set aside.
Combine flour, salt and pepper. Dip cubes steaks in buttermilk mixture, then
dredge in flour mixture. Let stand 10 minutes on paper towels. Pour oil to depth
of 1/4-inch in heavy skillet. Fry steaks in hot oil over medium—high heat, adding
oil as necessary until the meat is browned. Remove steaks from pan and drain
on paper towels. Use drippings to make cream gravy or serve steaks plain.

Note: Breadcrumbs or fine cracker crumbs may be added to flour mixture for
dredging.
Serves 6.

SUNDAY SUPPER MEATLOAF
"My mother always made this for Sunday supper."
Jon Whitehead–Billings

1 lb. **Ground Beef**
1 lb. **Sausage**
1 lg. **Onion,** chopped
1 lg. **Green Bell Pepper**, chopped
2 **Eggs**
1/3 cup **Ketchup**
1 cup **Cracker Crumbs**
1/2 tsp. **Garlic Powder**
1/2 tsp. **Onion Powder**
Salt and **Pepper** to taste
4 slices **Bacon**

Mix all ingredients together (except Bacon). Divide meat mixture and put into 2 loaf pans. Bake at 375 degrees for 40 minutes. Remove from oven; spread additional ketchup on top of each loaf; place 2 slices of bacon over ketchup on top of each loaf; place 2 slices of bacon over ketchup and return to oven for 20 minutes or until bacon is done.
Serves 6–8.

COWBOY FAJITAS

"I don't add anything to these fajitas— no lettuce, cheese, etc., just the ingredients listed." Dave Williams—Norman

1 1/2 lbs. **Cube Steak**
1 tbsp. **Oil**
1 **Onion**, chopped
1 **Green Bell Pepper**, diced
Salt and **Pepper** to taste
Garlic Power to taste
3/4 cup **Worcestershire Sauce**
Flour Tortillas (fajita size)
Butter or **Margarine**
Mustard

Cut cube steak into 1/2 inch by 2 inch strips. Heat skillet, add oil, then onion and bell pepper. Sauté until vegetables are almost tender; sprinkle with salt, pepper and garlic powder. Add steak strips and cook on high until all oil is cooked away. Add Worcestershire sauce and cook until sauce is nearly all gone; remove skillet from heat and cover for 5 minutes. In another skillet, add a small amount of butter or margarine and brown tortillas over low heat. Spread tortillas with a small amount of mustard, add meat and serve.
Makes 6–8 fajitas.

RANCH STROGANOFF

"This is a family recipe adapted to our hunting lodge. We have lots of deer and wild turkey hunters and they love to have wild meat used in recipes."
Lena Clancy—Deer Run Lodge & Hunting Preserve, Durant

2 lbs. **Vension Steak** *
6 tbsp. **Flour**
1 tsp. **Salt**
1/4 cup **Margarine**
1 tsp. **Pepper**
1/4 cup **Corn Oil**
2 cans (3 oz. ea.) **Mushrooms**
1/3 cup **Water**
2 pkgs. (1 oz. ea.) **Onion Soup Mix**
1 carton (16 oz.) **Sour Cream**
Cooked **Noodles** or **Rice**

Slice steak across grain into strips.** Combine flour and salt. Dredge meat in flour mixture. In a large skillet over medium heat; add margarine, pepper and oil; brown steak strips. Add mushrooms (include liquid) and water. Stir in soup mix. Bring to a boil, reduce heat; stir in sour cream. Cook over low heat, uncovered, until thoroughly heated. Serve over noodles or rice.
Serves 8.
*Porterhouse or sirloin steaks work well in this recipe too.
**Partially frozen steaks are easier to cut.

The Chisholm Trail
In its time, the Chisholm Trail was one of the wonders of the world. Originally a trading route developed by Jesse Chisholm, a part-Cherokee trader, The Chisholm Trail began at San Antonio, Texas and ended at Abilene, Kansas, roughly following present-day U.S. Hwy. 81. Cattle herds as large as 10,000 head and sometimes less than 10 miles apart were driven over the trail.

BIEROCKS

"This was originally a Russian recipe that was adopted by my German forebears when they lived there. Our family serves it with slices of watermelon." Sara Yauk–Buffalo

2 pkgs. **Dry Yeast**
2 cups warm **Milk**
1/4 cup plus 1 tbsp. **Brown Sugar**
1 tsp. **Salt**

1 **Egg**
1/4 cup **Margarine**
5 cups **Flour**

Dissolve yeast in milk. Add sugar, salt, egg and margarine. Mix well. Add flour gradually, mixing well. Knead and let rise until double in bulk. Roll dough out to 1/4 –inch thickness and cut into 5–inch squares. Place 3 tablespoons of Bierock Filling in the center of each square. Fold opposite corners to the center and pinch edges together. Place in a greased baking pan with seam sides down. Let rise about 20 minutes; then bake in a 350 degree oven until lightly browned. Brush top with soft **Butter**.
Makes 24 Bierocks.

BIEROCK FILLING

1 lb. **Ground Beef**
1 sm. head **Cabbage,** shredded
1 lg. chopped **Onion**
Salt and **Peppe**r to taste

In a skillet, heat ground beef slowly until cooked through. Add cabbage, onions, salt and pepper; cook until onions are tender. Do not brown.

Did You Know?
The Five Civilized Tribes (the Cherokee, Chickasaw, Choctaw, Creek and Seminole) were forced to move to Oklahoma between 1820 and 1842. These immigrant Indians were given the right to all of present-day Oklahoma except the Panhandle. Each tribe created its own nation and established its own legislature, courts and written laws, and built its own capital.

KATHIE'S CHICKEN FRIED STEAK
Kathie Stocksen—Enid

1 **Round Cube Steak**
1 **Egg**
1/3 cup **Milk**
Salt and **Pepper** to taste
1 cup **Flour**
Cooking Oil

Tenderize steak. Cut into serving size pieces. Beat egg and combine with milk: set aside. Combine salt, pepper and flour. Dredge meat in flour mixture and then in egg mixture. Let set for 10 minutes; then dredge again. Add cooking oil (3/4-inch deep) to a skillet and heat until very hot. Place meat in hot oil and brown 2–3 minutes; turn and brown the other side. Cover skillet and cook until juices run clear. Drain meat on paper towels.
Serves 4–6.

CHICKEN CASSEROLE
"This recipe came from a pre-school center attended by my youngest daughter, Heidi. It is my family's favorite casserole and it works great for our busy schedule." Teresa Wuerflein—Kremlin

1 pkg. (10 oz.) **Shell Macaroni**
1 can (10.75 oz.) **Cream Of Mushroom Soup**
1 tsp. **Seasoned Salt**
1 pint **Sour Cream**
3 cups grated **Cheddar Cheese**
1 **Chicken**, cooked, deboned and diced
1 cup crushed **Potato Chips**

Cook and drain macaroni; add rest of ingredients, except for potato chips. Place in a buttered casserole. Refrigerate overnight. Bake in 350 degree oven for 1 hour, uncovered, adding crushed potato chips during last 15 minutes. Freezes well. Serves 6–8.

GOULASH

"This recipe was given to me years ago by my mother-in-law."
Barbara Weatherwax-Enid

1 pkg. (10 oz.) **Macaroni**
2 qts. **Boiling Water**
2 tbsp. **Oil**
1/2 cup diced **Onion**
1/2 cup chopped **Green Bell Pepper**
1 cup **Water**
1 can (16 oz.) **Stewed Tomatoes**
1 can (15 oz.) **Tomato Sauce**
1 **Beef Bouillon Cube**
1 tsp. **Garlic Powder**
Salt to taste
1 cup grated **Colby Cheese**

Cook macaroni in boiling water until almost done; drain. Add oil to large skillet; braise beef over medium heat; drain. Add onion, bell pepper and water to skillet. Add stewed tomatoes, tomato sauce, bouillon cube, garlic powder and salt. Stir. Add macaroni to meat mixture and mix well. Place mixture in a casserole dish, top with grated cheese and bake in a 350 degree oven until macaroni is done and cheese has melted.
Serves 4-6.

Guthrie, the Capital of Oklahoma?
On November 16, 1907, Oklahoma became the 46th state in the Union. Charles N. Haskell of Muskogee was elected the first governor. The new state had a population of 55,849 and Guthrie was the first capital. Today, the Scottish Rite Temple sits on the site originally intended for the state capitol building. Oklahoma City became the state capital in 1910.

ENCHILADA CASSEROLE
"This recipe was the winner of the Mexican Foods Contest at the 1998 Garfield County Fair In Enid" Joyce Postier–Breckinridge

2 lbs. **Ground Beef**
1 med. chopped **Onion**
1 pkg. (6-inch) **Flour Tortillas**
2 cans (10.75 oz. ea.) **Cream Of Celery Soup**
1 can diced **Rotel® Tomatoes**
12 oz. cubed **Velveeta® Cheese**

In a skillet, sauté hamburger and onion. Drain. Spoon 2 tablespoons of meat mixture on each tortilla. Roll up and place in 9 x 13 glass baking dish. In microwaveable bowl, heat soup and tomatoes and melt cheese. Pour over tortillas. Bake in 350 degree oven for 20 minutes.
Serves 4–6.

BUFFALO SUMMER SAUSAGE
"We raised buffalo for over 20 years and enjoyed the leanness of the meat." Andrea Hutchison–Canton

2 lbs. **Ground Buffalo**
1 cup **Water**
1/4 tsp. **Garlic Salt**
1/4 tsp. **Pepper**
1/4 tsp. **Onion Salt**
2 tsp. **Liquid Smoke**
1 tbsp. **Mustard Seed**
2 tbsp. **Mortons® Tender Quick Salt**

Mix all ingredients together and divide into two rolls; wrap in double thickness of foil. Refrigerate for 24 hours. Bake at 450 degrees for 30 minutes; 300 degrees for 45 minutes; 250 degrees for 30 minutes; and 225 degrees for 30 minutes. Remove from oven and stand on end. Punch holes in foil to drain fats and juices. Sausages may be frozen after they cool.
Note: Do not substitute any other salt for the Morton's® Tender Quick Salt.

FRIED TUNA PATTIES

"This recipe is a favorite of mine, originally passed along to me by good friends as a gesture of friendship." Shirley Walton–Thayer–Enid

1 slice **White Bread**
1 lg. **Egg,** beaten
1 can (6oz.) **Tuna**
1/2 cup diced **Onion**

Soak bread in beaten egg then combine with tuna and onion in mixing bowl. Mix well; divide into 4 medium–sized patties. Fry patties in a large skillet coated with vegetable oil until they are lightly browned on one side; then flip to the other side and repeat. Drain patties on paper towels. Serve hot.
Serves 4.

KING RANCH CHICKEN

"This is really good." Stevana K. Sanford–Barnsdall

1 lg. whole **Chicken**
1 can (10.75 oz.) **Cream of Chicken Soup**
1 can (10.75 oz) **Cream of Mushroom Soup**
1 **Onion,** chopped
1 jar (12oz.) **Cheese Whiz®**
1 can **Rotel® Tomatoes**
1 cup cooked **Rice**, optional
1 pkg. grated **Longhorn Cheese**
1 pkg. **Flour Tortillas**

Boil chicken and debone, reserving broth. Over medium heat in a large saucepan, combine soups, onion, Cheese Whiz, tomatoes, rice and half of the grated cheese. Mix thoroughly; add chicken. Soak tortillas in chicken broth and layer in a 9 x 13 baking pan. Cover with half of chicken mixture. Repeat layer of tortillas and layer of chicken mixture. Top with remaining grated cheese. Bake in a 350 degree oven for 35 minutes.
Serves 4–6.

HOBO SUPPERS

"Wheat harvest time is hectic. The wheat must be cut and hauled to grain elevators before rains come, so no one has time for huge fancy meals. Food is often taken to the wheat fields in the trunk of a car and served on paper plates." Arlen Ediger—Enid

1 – 2 **Hamburger Patties** per person
Sliced **Potatoes**
Sliced **Carrots**
Pork 'N' Beans
Salt and **Pepper** to taste

Lightly brown hamburger patties in a skillet. Place each patty on a large square of aluminum foil. Top with 1 slice potato, 1 slice carrot and 2 tablespoons of pork 'n' beans. Add salt and pepper. Wrap patties in foil. Make as many packets as you need. Put packet on a flat baking pan or cookie sheet. Bake in a 350 degrees oven for 30 minutes or until potatoes and carrots are done. Remove from oven and serve immediately. Be careful, as they will be very hot when foil is first opened.

Boomers & Sooners

In the 1880's, the United States government bought over 3 million acres of land from the Creek and Seminole Indian tribes. At noon, on April 22, 1889, almost two million of those acres were opened for settlement. By evening of that day, about 50,000 "boomers" had moved into Oklahoma. Some settlers, called "sooners," went into the area early and opened claim to the best lands. To hide their duplicity, the Sooners ran their horses hard on the day of the opening so that the tired horses could be shown as proof of the validity of their claims to the other pioneers.

ENCHILADAS
Julia Bays–Alava

2 lbs. lean **Ground Beef**
3 tbsp. evaporated minced **Onion**
1 tsp. **Cumin**
2 tsp. **Garlic Powder**
2 cans (7oz.) diced **Green Chiles**

1 lb. **Velveeta® Cheese,** cubed
24 (6") **Flour Tortillas**
Velveeta® Cheese slices
1 can (19 oz.) mild **Red Enchilada Sauce**
1 can (19 oz.) **Green Enchilada Sauce**

Brown hamburger and drain. Add seasonings and green chiles. Melt Velveeta cheese into mixture. Divide meat mixture between tortillas and roll. Place tortillas in a baking dish. Place several slices of Velveeta over top. Pour enchilada sauces over all. Bake at 325 degrees for 20 minutes, or until heated through.
Serves 6–8.

RALPH'S BEER MEATLOAF
"This recipe is in memory of Ralph and Thelma Harris of Ralph's Spudnut and Restaurant. Ralph's was a popular hangout for teens in the 1950s-60s. It was located in central Oklahoma at the intersection of Highways 18 and 33. That intersection is known as 'the pipeline crossroads of the world."
Jeany Harris–Cushing

2 lbs. **Ground Chuck**
1 Egg
1 med. **Apple,** cored and chopped
1 lb. bulk **Pork Sausage**

1 small **Onion**, chopped
1 cup **Beer**
1/2 cup dry **Bread Crumbs**
1 cup **Applesauce**

Mix all ingredients together (except applesauce); blend well. Shape into loaf; put in loaf pan. Bake 30 minutes at 350 degrees, then spread applesauce over the entire loaf and continue baking another 30 minutes. Cool slightly, then slice and serve with additional hot applesauce on the side.
Serves 6–8.

SWEDISH MEATBALLS

"I've been preparing these meatballs for about 20 years—my mother always made them for summer parties or holiday get-togethers. The only problem is, there's never quite enough!" Bev Walton-Porter-Enid

1 1/2 lbs. lean **Ground Beef**
1 sm. **Onion,** diced
2 **Eggs,** beaten
1 cup crumbled **Cracker** or **Bread Crumbs**
1 jar (12oz.) **Heinz® Chili Sauce**
1 jar (10oz.) **Welch's Grape Jelly**
1/2 cup drained **Pineapple,** cubes or tidbits

In a large bowl, combine beef, onion, eggs and crackers or crumbs and mix well. Roll mixture into small (1-inch) balls. Arrange meatballs in a skillet coated with vegetable oil; brown on all sides. When done, remove from pan and drain on paper towels. Set crockpot on LOW; add chili sauce, jelly and pineapple tidbits. Mix well. Add meatballs and stir to coat them with sauce. Allow meatballs to simmer in crockpot for 3 to 4 hours, allowing sauce to marinate and cook through meatballs.
Serves 6-8.

Sequoyah's Home Site
Near Sallisaw is Sequoyah's home site, a log cabin that was built in 1829. Sequoyah, a Cherokee Indian who never learned English, gained world wide fame when he developed an alphabet using modified letters from English, Greek and Hebrew to represent the sounds in the Cherokee language. His aim was to record and preserve ancient tribal cultures. Thousand of Cherokees learned to read and write in their own language thanks to Sequoyah.

GREAT AUNT VERDA'S CHICKEN ENCHILADAS
"Use a bigger can of chiles for a spicier flavor."
J.B. Blosser Bittner—Woodward

2–3 lbs.**Chicken**
1 medium **Onion**, chopped
1 tsp. **Butter**
1 can (10.75 oz.) **Cream of Mushroom Soup**

1 can (10.75 oz.) **Cream of Chicken Soup**
1 can (4oz.) diced **Green Chiles**
18 soft **Corn Tortillas**
1 lb. grated **Cheese**

Place chicken in a saucepan, cover with water and boil until tender; reserve broth. Debone and cube chicken. In a large skillet, sauté onion in butter. Add soups, 1 1/2 cups chicken broth, chiles, and chicken. Heat through. In a large baking dish, alternate layers of tortillas, chicken mixture and grated cheese, ending with cheese on top. Bake in 350 degree oven for 30 minutes. Serves 4–6.

BAKED STEAK
"This is one of my family's favorite meat dishes."
Alberta Leierer—Ringwood

1 **Round Steak,** tenderized
1 cup **Flour**
1 tbsp. **Butter Flavor Crisco®**

1 cup **Water**
1 pkg. (2.5 oz.) **Onion Soup Mix**
1 cup sliced **Mushrooms**

Cut steak into serving–size pieces. Dredge well in flour. Heat Crisco® in a large skillet. Brown meat well on both sides. Place meat in a casserole dish and pour excess oil from skillet over top. Add 1 cup water* and onion soup mix to skillet; stir well, add mushrooms and heat to simmer. Pour soup mixture over the meat and bake at 350 degrees for 20–30 minutes.
Serves 4.

*For extra sauce for gravy, add another cup of water and a beef bouillon cube to the skillet.

MEXICAN CASSEROLE
"I got this from a neighbor and it's soooo good." Rosailla M. Fuksa–Bison

2 lbs. **Ground Beef**
1 lg. **Onion,** diced
1 diced **Green Bell Pepper**
Salt and **Pepper** to taste
1 can (10.75 oz.) **Cream Of Mushroom Soup**
1 can (10.75 oz.) **Cream Of Chicken Soup**
1 can (15 oz.) mild **Enchilada Sauce**
Drops of **Louisiana® Hot Sauce**, to taste
8 **Flour Tortillas**
1 cup grated **Sharp Cheddar Cheese**

Brown hamburger with onion, green pepper, salt and pepper. Drain well. Combine soups with the enchilada sauce. Stir in hot sauce. Add meat mixture to soup mixture and stir well. Layer 4 tortillas in the bottom of a 9 x 13 glass baking dish; spoon half of meat and soup mixture over top. Layer remaining tortillas and remaining meat and soup mixture. Sprinkle with cheese. Cover with foil and bake in a 350 degree oven for 1 hour.
Serves 6–8.

GERMAN HOT SANDWICH
"This is a perfect dish for a wheat harvest meal."
Helen Geminden–Carrier

2 lbs. **Ground Beef**
25 **Soda Crackers**
1/4 cup **Cream**
1 pkg. (8) **Hamburger Buns**

1 med. **Onion,** chopped
4–5 tbsp. **Mustard**
Salt and **Pepper** to taste

Crumble meat in a heavy saucepan. Add chopped onion; barely cover with water and boil. Continue to cook until the liquid cooks down. Stir in crackers and mustard. Add the cream, salt and pepper. Continue cooking, stirring occasionally until mixture has thickened. Serve on hamburger buns.
Serves 4.

FIREFIGHTER BEANS

Woodward has a combination paid and volunteer fire department. Marshall Bittner is a paid firefighter and the Woodward County Public Education officer. He presents fire and burn prevention programs to the county's schools and similar information for businesses and organizations. Bittner has been a member of the Woodward Fire Department for 20 years and is a part-time field instructor for the Oklahoma State University Fire Service Training Dept. He perfected these bean recipes a decade ago while coordinating a cookout to wrap up a training session for new firefighters: hence the use of fire fighting terminology. The beans have become a tradition with the completion of Fire Fighter One courses. "No firefighter believes there are beans too hot for him or her to eat," Bittner said. "After a few bites they rethink that position. It's all part of the learning process."

SMOKE CALL BEANS

"You can smell the smoke, but the fire is controlled in the incipient phase—the temperature of the reducing agent was lowered to below ignition point, therefore stopping the chemical chain reaction and leaving an adequate source of oxidizing agent. Most rookies can be trained to achieve knockdown on these beans."
Marshall Bittner—Woodward Fire Department, Woodward

1 lb. **Bacon,** diced
1 lb. **Onion,** diced
6 cans **Pork and Beans**
6 dashes of **Worcestershire Sauce**
3 dashes of **Liquid Smoke**

3/4 cup **Brown Sugar**
1 squirt (2–3oz.) **Mustard**
2 squirts (4–6 oz.) **Ketchup**
Small amount **Garlic,** minced
1 or 2 oz. **Jalapeño Peppers**
 (about 10 slices)

Fry bacon and onion; drain. Mix with remaining ingredients. Bake at 325 degrees for 1 to 2 hours.

FLASHOVER BEANS

"Conditions exist within these beans to cause flashover if proper extinguishment and ventilation procedures are not followed! There is plenty of fuel and lots of heat left in these beans. Full bunkout gear should be worn while eating them."
Marshall Bittner, Woodward Fire Department—Woodward

1 lb. **Bacon**, cut into small pieces
1 lb. **Onions,** chopped
6 cans (15 oz. ea.) **Pork and Beans**
6 dashes **Worcestershire Sauce**
3 dashes **Liquid Smoke**
1 squirt (2–3 oz.) **Mustard**
2 squirts (3–6 oz.) **Ketchup**
Moderate amount of **Garlic,** minced
20 Hot Jalapeño Peppers slices with a dash of juice

Fry bacon and onion; drain. Mix with other ingredients. Bake in 325 degree oven 1 to 2 hours.

FALSE ALARM BEANS

"No heat, no fire, never was, never will be. Save some of these for the Fire Chief." Marshall Bittner—Woodward Fire Department, Woodward

3/4 lb. **Bacon** diced
3/4 lb. **Onion** chopped
4 cans (15 oz. ea.) **Pork and Beans**
2 dashes **Liquid Smoke**
1 squirt (2–3 oz.) **Mustard**
2 squirts (3–6 oz.) **Ketchup**
1/2 cup **Brown Sugar**
Small amount **Garlic,** minced
4 dashes **Worcestershire Sauce**

Fry bacon and onion; drain. Add other ingredients and mix well. Bake in 325 degree oven 1 to 2 hours.

BACKDRAFT BEANS

"Full protective gear is required while preparing these. Ventilation is a must. These beans are in the smoldering phase. Once ignited, they will cook themselves. After consumption of beans, lethal amounts of carbon monoxide, carbon dioxide, hydrogen and methane are often given off by firefighters creating a toxic environment for those in the area."
Marshall Bittner—Woodward Fire Department, Woodward

1 lb. **Bacon,** diced
1 lb. strong **Onion,** diced
6 (15 oz.) cans **Ranch—Style Pinto Beans**
60 slices (about 12 oz.) **Jalapeño Peppers** with some juice
6 dashes **Tabasco®** or other **Hot Sauce**
3 dashes **Liquid Smoke**
6 dashes **Worcestershire Sauce**
1 squirt (2–3 oz.) **Mustard**
1/2 cup **Brown Sugar**
Small amount of **Garlic,** minced

Fry bacon and onion; drain. Mix with other ingredients. Bake in a 375 degree oven 1 to 2 hours.

Note: To avoid ill side effects caused by over consumption, have large quantities of homemade ice cream on hand at all times when these beans are being served.

Route 66
Stretching 400 miles across the entire state, from Quapaw in the northeast corner to Texola, near the Texas border, famed Route 66 also known as the "Mother Road," can still provide hardy travelers the chance to "get their kicks on Route 66."

Side Dishes

Recipe:_____

From:_____

Ingredients:_____ _____

_____ _____

_____ _____

_____ _____

_____ _____

Directions:_____

_____

_____

_____

_____

_____

Recipe:_____

From:_____

Ingredients:_____ _____

_____ _____

_____ _____

_____ _____

_____ _____

Directions:_____

_____

_____

_____

_____

_____

GRETCHEN'S SQUASH CASSEROLE
"I often serve this at the guest ranch."
Mary White–Island Guest Ranch–Ames

8 **Yellow Squash,** sliced
1 med. **Onion,** finely chopped
1 **Green Bell Pepper,** chopped
1 **Red Bell Pepper,** chopped

1 tbsp. **Butter**
1 1/2 cup grated **Mozzarella Cheese**
1 cup grated **Cheddar Cheese**
1 cup **Bread Crumbs**

Boil or steam squash until tender and drain. Sauté onion and peppers in butter until tender. Spread squash in a 9 x 13 casserole dish, cover with most of the cheese and 3/4 cup of pepper/onion mixture. Cover casserole with bread crumbs. Sprinkle top with a little cheese and remaining pepper mixture. Bake in 350 degree oven for 30 minutes or until cheese is melted and bread crumbs are browned.
Serves 4–6.

SCALLOPED CABBAGE
"My sister gave me this recipe. It's easy and any lover of cooked cabbage would enjoy it." Karen Barnes–Ames

1 head **Cabbage,** wedged
3 tbsp. **Onion,** chopped
Seasoned Salt and **Pepper** to taste
1 cup grated **Cheddar Cheese**
1 can (10.75 oz.) **Cream of Celery Soup**
Margarine
1/4 cup **Bread Crumbs**

In a greased casserole, layer the cabbage, onion, seasoned salt, pepper and cheese. Pour soup over all and dot with margarine. Sprinkle top with bread crumbs. Bake in a 400 degree oven for 30 minutes or until golden brown.
Serves 6–8.

SOUTHERN—STYLE BAKED CORN

"This recipe was passed down from my grandmother, Lucy Kelly, and I've been preparing it for about 45 years. It's a special favorite at Thanksgiving and Christmas." Shirley Walton–Thayer–Enid

2 cans (8.75 oz.ea.) **Whole Kernel Corn,** drained
1 lg. **Egg**, beaten
Salt and **Pepper** to taste
4 tsp. **Sugar**
1 cup **Milk**
Dash of **Paprika**

Mix all ingredients together (except paprika) in medium sized baking dish. Sprinkle paprika over top of mixture. Bake in a 350 degree oven for 45–60 minutes, or until mixture is set. Serves 6–8.

COUNTRY HARVEST POTATOES

"Everyone helps with the cooking for the wheat harvest crew which is usually from 8–10 men. Harvest season lasts about two weeks and two meals a day are taken to the wheat fields." Andrea Hutchison–Canton

1 pkg. (32oz.) frozen **Hash Browns**
1 can (10.75 oz.) **Cream of Chicken Soup**
1/2 soup can **Water**
1 med. **Onion,** diced
8 oz. **Shredded American Cheese**
1 1/2 tsp. **Salt**
8 oz. **Light Sour Cream**

Combine all ingredients in greased 9 x 13 baking dish. Top with **Corn Flake Topping**. Bake in a 350 degrees oven for 45 minutes.
Serves 8.

CORN FLAKE TOPPING

2 cups crushed **Corn Flakes**
1/4 cup melted **Butter**
Combine corn flakes and butter.

BREAD DRESSING

"This is a family favorite side dish and is especially good if pork chops are baked on top." Jane Spreier–Okeene

1 stick **Butter**
1 lg. **Onion,** chopped
1 cup diced **Celery**
1/2 cup **Water**
3 **Eggs,** beaten
2 cups **Chicken Broth, Milk** or **Water**
1 loaf stale **Bread,** cubed
Few pieces **Cornbread,** cubed
1 tsp. **Salt**
1 tbsp. **Celery Seed**
2 tbsp. **Sage** or **Poultry Seasoning**

In a saucepan, melt butter and add onion, celery and water. Cover and cook until onion is done but not brown. Beat together the eggs and broth (or milk or water). Combine all ingredients in a casserole dish, cover and bake 1 hour at 325 degrees. Serves 4 to 6.

FRIED GREEN TOMATOES

"My mother always made this during fresh tomato season. I still do, and it's a favorite of our family and friends." Jon Whitehead–Billings

6–8 lg. **Green Tomatoes**
2 **Eggs**
Salt and **Pepper** to taste
1/2 cup **Cooking Oil**
Flour

Wash, stem and slice unpeeled tomatoes about 1/2-inch thick. Beat eggs lightly, add salt and pepper and combine. In a skillet, heat oil over medium heat. Dip slices of tomato in egg mixture, then in flour, covering well. Cook tomatoes in hot oil in a skillet, turning when tender and brown.
Serves 4.

SPANISH RICE
"I've made this dish for years and my family loves it."
Betty Rathjen—North Enid

1 cup uncooked **Rice**
1 **Onion,** chopped
1 **Green Bell Pepper,** chopped
1 **Red Bell Pepper,** chopped
2 stalks **Celery,** chopped
3 cups canned or made with bouillon cubes, **Chicken Broth**
1 can (28 oz) **Tomatoes,** diced, undrained
1 tsp. **Oregano**
1/2 tsp. **Tumeric**
1 **Bay Leaf**
1 lb. fresh **Mushrooms,** sliced
1 can (15 oz.) **Peas,** drained
1/4 cup **Lemon Juice**
Freshly ground **Black Pepper**

Combine rice, onion, peppers, celery, broth, tomatoes and seasonings, bring to a boil; simmer 30 minutes, covered. Add mushrooms and simmer 10 minutes. Stir in peas and simmer 5 minutes. Stir in lemon juice and pepper to taste. Remove bay leaf before serving.
Serves 6–8.

CORN PUDDING
"This is my grandmother's recipe. The original version starts out with 'butter, the size of an egg'." Mary Frances Myers—Tulsa

1/4 cup **Butter**
1 can (14.75 oz.) **Cream Style Corn**
2 1/2 tbsp **Sugar**

1 tbsp. **Cornstarch**
3 **Eggs,** beaten
2 1/2 cups **Milk**

Melt butter in a baking dish. Mix corn, sugar, cornstarch and egg yolks; add milk and beaten egg whites. Bake 1/2 hour at 350 degrees or until set.
Serves 4

FAMILY RECIPES

"These three recipes have been in my family since the Cherokee Strip Land Run. They were the first dishes I learned to cook."
Iilene Whitehead–Drummond

FRIED POTATOES

6–8 lg. **Potatoes**   1 lg. **Onion**, diced
1/2 cup **Cooking Oil**   **Salt** and P**epper** to taste

Peel and slice potatoes. In a heavy skillet, heat oil over medium–high heat. Add potatoes, onions, salt and pepper. Stir to coat all potatoes with oil. Cover skillet with lid; turn down heat to medium and cook until tender. Remove lid and turn up heat to brown potatoes. Serves 4.

FRIED SWEET POTATOES

3 to 4 large **Sweet Potatoes,** peeled
1/3 cup **Cooking Oil**
Salt and **Pepper** to taste

Slice potatoes 1/2-inch thick into saucepan. Add water to cover. Boil approximately 10 minutes or until only slightly cooked. Drain and let cool. Heat oil in a skillet; add sweet potatoes, salt and pepper. Cover. Cook until tender and brown.
Serves 4.

FRIED APPLES

10–12 cooking **Apples**   1 cup **Sugar**
1/3 cup **Cooking Oil**   1/4 cup **Cinnamon**

Wash, core and slice apples. Heat oil in a heavy skillet over medium–high heat. Add apples to hot oil, stirring occasionally. Cook until tender. Add sugar and cinnamon; stir frequently for 5 to 10 minutes or until thoroughly heated.
Serves 6

GOLDEN CORN—CHEESE CASSEROLE

"My good friend, Dorotha Keller—Foffman, brought this casserole to our Fellowship Dinner one Sunday in the 1960's. I liked it so much I asked her for the recipe. It quickly becomes a family favorite and is often made when the family gets together." Jean Long—Garber

2 cups **Whole Kernel Corn**
2 tbsp. grated **Onion**
1/4 cup chopped **Celery**
1 cup crushed **Soda Crackers**
1/2 cup **American Cheese,**
   cut in 1/2" squares

2 tbsp **Salad Oil**
1/2 tsp. **Salt**
3 **Egg Yolks,** well beaten
1 1/2 cups **Milk**
3 **Egg Whites**, beaten until stiff

In a medium bowl, mix all ingredients (except egg whites) in order given. Stir well. Fold in the egg whites. Pour mixture into a greased 8 x 11 baking dish. Bake at 350 degrees for 40 minutes or until the center is firm and a light brown color. This will fall somewhat after removal from the oven. Serve as soon as possible. Serves 6.

GREAT GRANDMA STIVENSON'S DILL PICKLES

"I used to help my Grandmother Crooks make these when I was a little girl. The recipe has been used by five generations of our family." Jeany Harris —Cushing

2 bunches **Dill**
1 **Hot Pepper**
1 clove **Garlic**

1/2 tsp. **Alum**
1 tsp. **Mustard Seed**
med. size **Cucumbers**, scrubbed

To each sterilized quart jar, add dill, hot pepper, garlic, cucumbers, alum and mustard seed. Stand cucumbers on end to fill. Cover with boiling **Pickle Brine**. Seal jars.

PICKLE BRINE

1 cup **Vinegar**   2 cups **Water**   1 tbsp. **Salt**
Combine all ingredients in a saucepan and bring to a boil.

CHOW CHOW
(Vegetable Relish)
"My mother taught me how to make this."
Gene Herren–Romona

1 qt. **Green Tomatoes**
6 small **Onions**
3 **Green Bell Peppers**
3 **Red Bell Peppers**
1 small head **Cabbage**

Brine:
1/4 cup **Salt**
1 qt. **Water**
2 cups **Vinegar**
2 cups **Sugar**

Chop vegetables into small pieces; place in a large bowl. Create brine by mixing salt and water, pour over vegetables and allow to stand overnight. Place vegetables in a colander and drain for 1 hour. Place vegetable mixture in a saucepan: add vinegar and sugar. Heat to boiling point and simmer for 1/2 hour, stirring frequently. May be refrigerated or canned.

Enid
Enid was born overnight with the opening of the Cherokee Outlet to white settlement. At noon on Sept. 16, 1893, the greatest horse race in history occurred. Some 100,000 settlers raced for the best 160-acre sections of land in what had been the Cherokee Strip.

Recipe: _____

From: _____

Ingredients: _____ _____

_____ _____

_____ _____

_____ _____

_____ _____

_____ _____

Directions: _____

_____

_____

_____

_____

_____

Recipe: _____

From: _____

Ingredients: _____ _____

_____ _____

_____ _____

_____ _____

_____ _____

_____ _____

Directions: _____

_____

_____

_____

_____

_____

BREADS

PINEAPPLE—ZUCCHINI BREAD
"This freezes well, which comes in handy if it's a big zucchini year in the garden. The pineapple adds a different, sweet twist and additional moistness." Kate Morrison—Enid

3 **Eggs,** beaten
1 cup **Salad Oil**
2 cups **Sugar**
2 tsp. **Vanilla**
2 cups shredded **Zucchini**
1 can (8 oz.) crushed **Pineapple**, drained
3 cups **Flour**

2 tsp. **Baking Soda**
1 tsp. **Salt**
1/2 tsp. **Baking Powder**
1 1/2 tsp. **Cinnamon**
1 cup chopped **Walnuts**
1 cup **Currants**

Beat together eggs, salad oil, sugar and vanilla until foamy. Stir in zucchini and pineapple. Sift flour with remaining dry ingredients and stir until just blended. Add walnuts and currants. Pour into two greased and floured loaf pans. Bake at 350 degrees for 1 hour. Makes 2 loaves.

FUNNEL CAKES
Central Junior H. S. Home Economics Classes—Sand Springs
Courtesy of Oklahoma Wheat Commission, Oklahoma City

2 **Eggs,** beaten
1 1/2 cups **Milk**
2 cups **Flour**
1 tsp. **Baking Powder**

1/2 tsp. **Salt**
1 cup **Cooking Oil**
Powdered Sugar

In a mixing bowl, combine eggs and milk. Sift together flour, baking powder and salt. Add to egg mixture; beat until smooth. Test the mixture to see if it flows easily through a funnel. Heat oil to 360 degrees. Place batter in funnel while holding your finger over the end. Drop batter into hot oil in a spiral shape. Cook until lightly browned, turn and cook the other side. Drain on paper towels. Dust with powdered sugar.
Makes 6–8 cakes.

CINNAMON STICK BUNS
"These are a family favorite." Julia Bays–Alva

11/4 cups **Milk**
3 cups **Flour**
3 tbsp. **Sugar**
1 tsp. **Salt**

3 tbsp. **Butter**
2 tsp. fast rising **Yeast***
1/3 cup **Butter**
2 tsp. **Cinnamon**

Mix milk, flour, sugar, salt, 3 tablespoons butter and yeast together. Knead and let rise until doubled in bulk (about one hour). Punch down dough and turn onto floured surface. It will be very sticky. Roll into a 16 x 10 rectangle. Spread 1/3 cup butter over top and sprinkle with cinnamon. Roll dough up jellyroll–style and pinch seams together. Cut into 1 1/2 inch thick slices and place each slice in pan on top of **Sticky Sauce.** Let dough double in size (about an hour). Bake at 375 degrees for 20–25 minutes. Cool for no more than 3 minutes, then invert pan so sauce and nuts are on top of buns when served.

*Or 3 tsp. active dry yeast

STICKY SAUCE

1/2 cup **Butter**
1 cup **Brown Sugar**
1/2 cup **Corn Syrup**
1 cup **Pecans**

Warm butter, sugar and syrup over medium heat until sugar dissolves. Spread sauce on the bottom of a 13 x 9 baking pan and sprinkle with pecans.

ZWIEBACK

"On Saturday mornings the house smelled of fresh, warm bread. That's when the Mennonite mothers would make the two-layered rolls called Zwieback. They were baked on Saturday so they would be ready to serve after church on Sunday at lunchtime. When Mennonites immigrated to America from Prussia and Russia in 1875, they ate Zwieback to keep alive. My mother continues that baking tradition. This is her recipe."
Arlene Ediger—Enid

2 cups **Milk**
1 cup **Potato Water**
2 tbsp. **Margarine**
1/3 cup **Sugar**
2 1/2 tsp. **Salt**
2 pkgs. **Dry Yeast**
3-5 cups **Flour**

Combine milk, potato water and margarine in a small saucepan. Heat until margarine is melted. Let cool a bit. In a large bowl, combine sugar and salt. Pour milk mixture into bowl and stir. Let mixture cool to 100-115 degrees. (If it is too hot it will kill the yeast. If it's too cool, the yeast won't activate.) Add yeast to liquid mixture. Stir. Mix in 3 cups of flour. Continue to add flour and mix until dough is stiff. Knead dough on a flour-covered board or counter top until smooth. Place dough in a greased bowl, cover and put in warm place. Let it rise until doubled in size. Remove dough from bowl and punch down and knead again a few times. Grease 2 flat cookie sheets. Pinch off small, egg-size balls of dough and place on cookie sheet. Pinch off smaller balls the size of a 50-cent piece or large marble. Place the small ball on top of the larger ball and push together with your index finger. Let rolls rise until double. Bake at 350 degrees until brown.
Yields 3-4 dozen.

BLOSSOM COFFEE CAKE
Grand champion winner in the senior division/sweet breads category of the Wheatheart Bread Baking Contest at the State Fair.
Betty Stejskal—Yukon
Courtesy of Oklahoma Wheat Commission, Oklahoma City

2 pkg. **Yeast**
1 tbsp. **Sugar**
1/3 cup **Warm Water**
3/4 cup **Half and Half**
1/2 cup **Margarine**
1/2 cup **Sugar**
Salt to taste
3 **Eggs,** beaten
5 cups **Flour**

FILLING:
Jam of your choice

GLAZE:
1 cup **Powdered Sugar**
2 tbsp. **Milk**

In a bowl, dissolve yeast and 1 tablespoon sugar in warm water. In a saucepan, heat half and half, margarine, 1/2 cup sugar and salt until warm. Combine with yeast mixture. Add eggs; mix well. Gradually add flour. Knead; place in a greased bowl. Cover; let rise until doubled. Punch down; divide into 21 equal pieces. Roll each piece into a 7-inch rope. Twist and form into a coil; tuck ends under. Place coil in center of greased baking sheet. Arrange 6 other coils around center coil, almost touching. Repeat with balance of dough. Cover and let rise until doubled. Punch center down. Place 1 tablespoon of jam in the center of each coil and bake at 350 degrees for 15–20 minutes or until golden brown. Combine glaze ingredients and drizzle over cakes when cool. Makes 3 coffee cakes.

BEST EVER CINNAMON ROLLS
Rosailla Fuksa–Bison

1 pkg. (4.6 oz.) **Vanilla Pudding Mix***
1 1/2 cups **Milk**
1 tsp. **Salt**
2 pkgs. **Yeast**
1/2 cup **Warm Water**

2 **Eggs,** beaten
Flour
1 stick **Margarine,** softened
1/2 cup **Brown Sugar**
1 tsp. **Cinnamon**

Cook pudding mix with milk; add salt. Let cool to lukewarm. In a large bowl, dissolve yeast in warm water. Add eggs and pudding mixture. Add enough flour (1–2 cups) to make a soft dough. Turn out onto a floured board. Knead until smooth, adding more flour as necessary. Let rise until double; punch down; let rise again. Turn out on a floured board and roll out. Spread top of dough with margarine. Combine cinnamon and brown sugar and sprinkle over top. Cut into rolls. Place on lightly greased 9 x 12 pan. Let rise. Bake at 350 degrees for 25 minutes.
*Not instant pudding

AUNT JAN'S FRUITY MUFFINS
"If you are watching fat content, add only half the amount of oil or substitute the required amount of oil with additional applesauce."
Jan Wood–Aunt Jan's Cozy Cottage B&B, Spiro

1/2 cup **Flour**
1 box (18.25 oz.) **Muffin Mix**
  with canned blueberries
Oil
Water

Egg
1/2 cup **Applesauce**
1–2 **Apples,** grated
3/4 cup **Nuts**
3/4 cup **Raisins**

Blend flour into muffin mix. Add oil, water and egg according to box instructions. Add applesauce. Stir just until blended. Gently fold in rinsed blueberries. Add apples, nuts and raisins. Bake in greased muffin pans at 400 degrees until golden brown.

REFRIGERATOR HOT ROLLS

**Senior division, dinner rolls category, winner of statewide Oklahoma
Wheatheart Bread Baking Contest. Gene Matli–Watonga
Courtesy of Oklahoma Wheat Commission, Oklahoma City**

2 pkgs. **Yeast**
2 cups hot **Water**
2 cups **Whole Wheat Flour**
2 tbsp. **Sugar**
1/2 cup **Honey**

1 tsp. **Salt**
1 **Egg,** beaten
1/2 cup **Oil**
5 cups **Bread Flour**

Dissolve yeast in water. Add whole wheat flour, sugar, honey and salt. Beat until
smooth. Add egg and oil; continue beating. Add bread flour, 1 cup at a time,
beating after each addition. Mix until soft (but not sticky) dough is formed. Place
in a greased bowl, turning to grease top. Cover; let rise for 1 hour. Shape into
dinner rolls. Bake at 350 degrees for 15–20 minutes.
Note: You can place a wet cloth over dough and store it in your refrigerator for
up to a week.

THE VERY BEST BREAD MACHINE BREAD

**"My Aunt gave me this recipe. I make up package of the dry mix so they
are ready when I need them." Lillian Porter–Enid**

Dry mix:
1 3/4 cups **Bread Flour**
3/4 cup **Whole Wheat Flour**
1 1/3 tsp. **Salt**

4 tsp. **Sugar**
1 1/2 tbsp. **Dry Milk**
2 tbsp. **Yeast**

Add:
1 cup plus 1 tbsp. **Water**
2 tbsp. **Honey**
2 tbsp**. Butter**

Combine all ingredients and place in bread machine. Cook according to
manufacturer's directions.

INDIAN FRY BREAD OR TACOS

"I learned to make this bread many years ago while working in an Indian school near Cortez, Colorado." Marie Sutton—Enid

4 cups **Flour**
1 1/2 cups **Water**
3 tsp. **Baking Powder**
3 tbsp. **Oil**
Salt to taste
Oil for frying
Cooking Spray

Mix all ingredients together to make a soft dough. Let dough set overnight or fry it immediately. Pinch off balls about the size of a golf ball. Place each roll between sheets of waxed paper that have been sprayed with cooking spray. Press or roll out very thing (about the size of a saucer). Put 1 inch of oil in a skillet and heat to 350 degrees. Fry bread until brown on one side; turn, brown the other side. Drain on paper towels. Serve warm with jam, jelly, honey or butter.

For tacos; make your favorite chili using taco seasoning instead of chili powder. Thicken chili or use slotted spoon to put chili on fry-bread. Add toppings of your choice.
Suggested toppings include: **Sour Cream**, grated **Cheese**, chopped **Onions** and **Tomatoes**, diced **Avocados**, **Black Olives** and **Picante Sauce.**

Ardmore
Fishing, boating and picnicking opportunities abound in the Ardmore area, provided by four municipal lakes—Ardmore City Lake, Lake Jean Neustadt, Mountain Lake and Rock Creek Reservoir. Just 20 miles southeast of Ardmore lies Lake Murray State Park, Oklahoma's largest state park.

SWEET DOUGH

When I was growing up the children would always ask for coffee bread and coffee like the adults had. Of course we would be served about an inch of coffee in a full glass of milk, but we were happy as larks and would just dunk away. I often make this sweet dough recipe into coffee bread."
Helen Geminden–Carrier

2 pkgs. **Yeast** (2 tbsp.)
3 cups **Warm Water**
2/3 cup **Sugar**
2 **Eggs,** beaten
1 1/2 tbsp. **Salt**
1/3 cup melted and cooled **Shortening**
8 cups **Flour**

Dissolve yeast in 1 cup warm water. Set aside. In a large bowl, mix sugar and remaining 2 cups water. Whisk in eggs; add salt and shortening. Alternately add yeast mixture and flour to sugar mixture, a little at a time. Work into a sticky dough. Dough will not be as stiff as bread dough and will require no kneading. It may be kept in the refrigerator up to a week, punching down as needed. When ready to bake, let rise at room temperature until twice the original size. Punch down and make Coffee Bread or just plain hot rolls as needed.

COFFEE BREAD

Make **Sweet Dough** recipe. Grease 8x8-inch pans. Roll dough out to 3/8-inch thickness. Place in pan leaving an inch of space all the way around. Spread with melted **Butter**; sprinkle with **Raisins** and a combination of **Brown Sugar**, **White Sugar** and **Cinnamon**. Pick up each corner of dough and bring to overlap at center; press gently to seal. Turn over and sprinkle top with **Granulated Sugar** and **Cinnamon**. Poke several holes almost to bottom with fingers. Pour **1 cup Cream** over top; cover with a towel and let rise. Bake about 30 minutes at 375 degrees or until brown. Turn onto a plate and scrape the thickened juice out onto the bread. Turn back over on a buttered serving dish.

APPLE FRITTERS
"These are really good! My guests usually clean up the platter."
Kay Kindt–Sharpe House Bed & Breakfast, Checotah

3 lg. **Jonathan Apples,** cored and sliced into 1/4" thick rings
Batter:
1 1/3 cup **Flour**
1/4 tsp. **Salt**
3 tbsp. **Sugar**
1 **Egg**
3 tbsp. **Cooking Oil**
2/3 cup **Milk**
1/2 tsp. **Cinnamon**
Dash of **Nutmeg**

Combine batter ingredients and stir until smooth. Dip apple rings in batter to cover both sides. Cook on a lightly oiled griddle or in a large skillet, turning to brown on both sides. Dust lightly with powdered sugar and serve immediately. Serves 4

MUFFINS
"I joined a 4–H club when I was nine years old. This was one of the first bread I learned to make. It is a long–time family favorite."
Mary Beth Lilley–Enid

2 cup **Flour**
3 tsp. **Baking Powder**
2 tbsp. **Sugar**
1 tsp. **Salt**
1 cup plus 1 tbsp**. Milk**
1 **Egg,** well beaten
2 tbsp. melted **Butter**

Sift dry ingredients together. Add milk to egg and melted butter and stir. Combine mixtures. Stir only enough to mix ingredients slightly. Batter will be lumpy. Spoon batter into greased muffin pans, filling about two–thirds full. Bake at 425 degrees for 15 to 20 minutes. Remove from pans at once. For richer, more cake–like muffins, double the amounts of sugar and butter. Makes 9 large or 18 small muffins.

APRICOT RING

Senior division/sweet breads category winner of the statewide Oklahoma
Wheathearts Bread Baking Contest. Penny Harnett—Fairview
Courtesy of Oklahoma Wheat Commission, Oklahoma City

Filling
1 cup dried diced **Apricots**
1 cup **Apple Juice**
3/4 cup **Sugar**

Dough:
1 pkg. active **Dry Yeast**
4 tbsp. divided **Sugar**
1 cup **Warm Water** (110 degrees)
4 cups divided **Flour**
1 tsp. **Salt**
2 **Eggs,** beaten
1/4 cup softened **Butter**
1 **Egg White,** lightly beaten
2 tbsp. sliced **Almonds**

In a saucepan, combine apricots and apple juice and place over medium heat.
Cover and cook about 12 minutes, stirring occasionally until apricots are tender
and juice is absorbed. Stir in sugar. Cook for 3 minutes, stirring constantly until
mixture is a thick paste. Cool. In large electric mixer bowl, dissolve yeast and
1 tablespoon of sugar in warm water. Let stand for 10 minutes. Add remaining
sugar, 1 cup flour and salt. Beat for 3 minutes. Add eggs, butter and remaining
flour to form a soft dough. Knead on a lightly floured surface for 10 minutes
or until smooth, adding flour if necessary to prevent sticking. Cover; let rest
20 minutes. Roll into an 18 x 11-inch rectangle on a lightly floured surface.
Spread filling over dough. Starting with the long side, roll up jellyroll—style; seal
edge. Form into a ring and place on a greased baking sheet. Cut ring at 1—inch
intervals, two—thirds of the way through, turning and pulling each slice outward
to form a petal. Cover with damp cloth; let rise in a warm place for 45 minutes
or until doubled in size. Brush with egg white and sprinkle with almonds. Bake at
350 degrees for 30 minutes or until browned. Makes 1 ring.

BASIC BREAD DOUGH

"Use this recipe to make Kraut Beirux, Cherry Kolaches and Blackberry Cougar." Andrea Hutchison—Chain Ranch, Canton

3 cups **Lukewarm Water**
3 tbsp. **Yeast**
1 tbsp. **Sugar**
Mix all together; let set until bubbly.

Add:
1 tsp. **Salt**
1/2 cup **Sugar***
Mix salt, sugar and yeast mixture together.
5–6 cups **Flour**

Add 5 cups flour and knead. Continue adding flour and kneading (1–2 minutes) until dough is no longer sticky.
*Note: Use 1 1/2 cups sugar for **Kraut Beirux**, 1 cup sugar for **Cherry Kolaches** or **Blackberry Cougar**.

KRAUT BEIRUX

1 med **Cabbage,** chopped
1 med. **Onion,** chopped
1 lb. **Ground Beef**
Salt and **Pepper** to taste

In a skillet, combine all ingredients and cook slowly until the cabbage is done. Make Basic Bread recipe and roll dough 1/4 to 1/2-inch thickness. Cut into squares. Place as much of the cooled cabbage mixture onto each square as desired, allowing enough space to pinch or seal sides together when doubled over. Place on greased cookie or cake pans. Allow to rise until double, about 30 minutes. Bake in 400 degree oven until brown.

CHERRY KOLACHES

Using **Basic Bread** recipe, make dough balls the size of plums or smaller and put them on a greased cookie sheet. Push down center of dough until flat. Let rise for about 30 minutes; add **Cherry Pie Filling** to the center of each. Bake for 15–20 minutes at 375 degrees. Let cool for 5 minutes and then drizzle with glaze. Sprinkle tops with **chopped Pecans** if desired.

Glaze:
1 cup **Powdered Sugar**
1/3 cup **Milk**
1 tsp. **Vanilla** or **Almond Extract**
Combine all ingredients and stir until smooth.

BLACKBERRY COUGAR

Make **Basic Bread** recipe on previous page. Spread dough out on a cookie sheet like pizza dough. Let rise for 30 minutes. Thaw and drain frozen **Blackberries** or **Dewberries** and spread over dough. Drizzle glaze over all and bake at 375 degrees until lightly brown.

Glaze:
1 cup **Sugar**
1/2 cup **Flour**
1/2 cup **Whipping Cream**
Combine all ingredients and stir until smooth.

Anadarko
Home to Indian City USA, this city features the only authentic restoration of Native American dwellings and way of life in America. Four annual Indian ceremonials are held at Indian City USA each year.

SOUR DOUGH STARTER
"You can make pancakes, biscuits and bread with this starter. "
Norma Kirby—Lamont

2 pkgs. **Active Yeast**
4 cup **Lukewarm Water** (110–115 degrees)
4 cups unsifted **Flour**

Put yeast in glass bowl. Add about 1/2 cup water. Use wooden spoon and stir to dissolve. Add remaining water alternately with flour. Stir well after each addition. Cover bowl with towel; place in warm place (85 degrees) 6 hours or overnight. Starter is then ready to use. It will look bubbly and a clear liquid will come to the top. Stir before measuring. Cover and refrigerate unused portion. Replenish starter at least once a week by stirring in 1/2 cup warm water and 1/2 cup flour. Cover, let stand overnight. Next morning stir down, cover and refrigerate. May be stored indefinitely.

SOURDOUGH BISCUITS
2 cups **Flour**
1 tsp. **Salt**
1/2 tsp. **Baking Soda**
1 tsp. **Baking Powder**
1/2 cup **Butter**
1/2 cup **Buttermilk**
1 cup **Sourdough Starter** (above)
Melted **Butter**

Combine dry ingredients: cut in butter. Combine starter and buttermilk; blend well. Stir this into crumb mixture with a fork. Form a soft dough. Turn out on floured surface. Knead 30 seconds. Roll 1/2-inch thick; cut into 3-inch rounds. Brush with butter. Cover with towel. Let stand in warm place 30 minutes. Bake in 425 degree oven 12–15 minutes.

Desserts

Oklahoma Pecan Cake
Grape-Tapioca Pudding
Chocolate Trifle
Sod House Date Pudding
Pawtucktzy
Egg Custard
Caramel Dumplings
Chocolate Pie

Poertzelki
Blue Ribbon Sugar Cookies
Spudnuts
Chocolate Chip Cookies
Ice Box Cookies
Smazenky

Baklava
Grandma Frey's Christmas Cookies
Jim's No-Bake Cookies
Mom's Chocolate Pie
Peanut Butter Bars
Ruth's Rhubarb Pie &
Foolproof Pie Crust
Pfeffernuesse
Mama's Prune Cake
Quick & Easy Ice Cream
Burnt Sugar Cake
Lill's Blue Ribbon Chocolate Cake
Chocolate Frosting
Fruit Cocktail
Pudding Cake
Shoo-fly Pie
Inez's Oatmeal Cake
Lemon Chiffon Pie
Candy Cane Coffee Cake
Turner Falls Inn Sheath Cake
Apricot Dessert
Cherry Angel Food Cake

Recipe: _____

From: _____

Ingredients: _____ _____

_____ _____

_____ _____

_____ _____

_____ _____

Directions: _____

_____

_____

_____

_____

_____

Recipe: _____

From: _____

Ingredients: _____ _____

_____ _____

_____ _____

_____ _____

_____ _____

Directions: _____

_____

_____

_____

_____

_____

BANANA BRAN MUFFINS
"Our guests enjoy these a lot."
Jennifer Kisling, Maple Place Bed & Breakfast–Enid

1 cup **Flour**
1 cup finely crushed **Bran Flakes**
1 tsp. **Baking Soda**
1/2 tsp. **Salt**
1/2 cup **Pecans**

2 ripe **Bananas**, mashed
1/2 cup softened **Butter**
1/2 cup **Brown Sugar**
1 **Egg**

In medium bowl, mix together flour, bran flakes, baking soda, salt and pecans. Set aside. In another bowl, beat together bananas and butter until curdled-looking; add brown sugar and egg. Beat until completely mixed. Add the dry ingredients and stir just until blended. Spoon into greased muffin tins, filling to three-quarters full. Bake at 375 degrees for 15–20 minutes. Makes 10 muffins.

BLUE RIBBON SUGAR COOKIES
"This recipe has won first place in many country fairs."
Kaylan Lawson–Oklahoma City

1/2 cup **Butter**
1/2 cup **Powdered Sugar**
1/2 cup **Sugar**
2 1/2 cup **Flour**
1/2 tsp. **Baking Soda**

1/2 tsp. **Cream Of Tartar**
1/4 tsp. **Salt**
1/2 cup **Oil**
1 **Egg,** beaten
1 tsp. **Vanilla**

Preheat oven to 350 degrees. In a large bowl, cream the butter and sugars together. Sift together flour, baking soda, cream of tartar and salt. Add oil, egg, vanilla and dry ingredients to creamed mixture. Mix thoroughly. Chill, then roll into 1-inch balls and place on an ungreased cookie sheet. Press with cookie press or bottom of glass that has a design on it. Bake in 350 degree oven for 10–12 minutes.
Makes about 4 dozen cookies.

OKLAHOMA PECAN CAKE

"My mother and my mother—in—law taught me to cook. This is a favorite cake that is great for all occasions, especially the holidays."
Gene Herren—Romona

1/2 cup **Butter Flavor Crisco®**
1/2 cup **Margarine**
6 **Eggs**
2 oz. **Lemon Extract**
1 cup **White Sugar**
1 cup **Brown Sugar**

2 cups **Flour,** divided
4 slices chopped **Candied Pineapple**
1/2 lb. **Candied Red** and **Green Cherries**
1 lb. chopped **Pecans**
1 tsp. **Baking Powder**

Cream together the Crisco, margarine, eggs, lemon extract and sugars. In separate bowls, combine 1 cup flour, pineapple, and candied cherries; remaining 1 cup flour, raisins, pecans and baking powder. Mix bowl contents, one at a time, with the creamed mixture. Place batter in a Bundt pan. Bake at 250 degrees for 2 1/2 hours or until tests done.

GRAPE—TAPIOCA PUDDING

"This was the most requested dessert when my grandmother came for Sunday dinner." Glenda Riddle—The Homestead Bed & Breakfast at GT Ranch—Red Rock

1 cup **Minute Tapioca**
1 qt. **Grape Juice**
1 cup **Sugar**
1/2 cup **Orange Juice**

1 cup chopped **Pecans**
1 1/2 cup crushed **Pineapple**
Vanilla Wafers

Measure grape juice and tapioca into a heavy saucepan. Cook, stirring often. The tapioca will take about 20 minutes to thicken. Add the sugar slowly and stir until dissolved. Take off the stove and let cool. Add 1/2 cup orange juice, the chopped pecans and crushed pineapple with juice. Mix well. Pour into an attractive glass serving dish and line the edges with vanilla wafers.

CHOCOLATE TRIFLE
Wynona Kuhnemund–Lahoma

1 pkg. **Chocolate Cake Mix**
2 boxes (4 oz. ea.) **Instant Chocolate Pudding Mix**
8 **Heath®** or **Skor® Candy Bars,** frozen and crumbled
1/2 cup **Kahlúa**
12 oz. thawed **Cool Whip®**

Bake cake according to package directions. (I prefer to use a 9 x 13 cake pan for this recipe.) Cool cake completely. Prepare chocolate pudding and allow it to set. Layer half of the cake (broken into large chunks) in a punch or trifle bowl. Pour 1/4 cup of the kahlúa over cake. Add a layer of half of the pudding, half of the candy bars and half of the Cool Whip. Repeat layers. Refrigerate overnight for the best results.

SOD HOUSE DATE PUDDING
"This recipe was handed down from my ancestors on my mother's side of the family. They came from the Midwest to Kansas and then into Oklahoma before statehood. My mother was born in a sod house in the Oklahoma panhandle, the portion called 'No Mans Land.' This dessert adapted very well to primitive cooking methods. It could be cooked in a Dutch oven over water, on top of a stove, or over water in wood– or cowchip– fired ovens. This dessert was a special treat, served mostly during holidays."
A.J. Rexroat–Heritage Manor Bed & Breakfast–Aline

1 cup **Brown Sugar**
1 cup **Hot Water**
1 cup **Sugar**
1 cup **Flour**
2 tsp. **Baking Powder**
1 cup **Milk**
1 tsp. **Vanilla**
1 cup chopped **Walnuts**
1/2 cup chopped **Dates**
Sprinkle of **Nutmeg**

Dissolve brown sugar in hot water in a 9 x 9 baking dish or pan. In a bowl, stir together white sugar, flour and baking powder. Add milk, vanilla, walnuts and dates; stir. Pour mixture over brown sugar and water mixture; do not stir. Bake at 325 degrees fairly firm to the touch. Serve with whipped cream, ice cream or cream, topped with a sprinkle of nutmeg.

PAWTUCKTZY

"This is one of my very favorite recipes because it's so easy to make and delicious. It always gets praise."
Sweet Pea Abernathy—Altus

4 squares **Semi—Sweet Chocolate**
2 sticks **Margarine**
2 cups **Sugar**
1 cup **Nuts**

4 **Eggs**
1 cup plus 2 tbsp. **Flour**
2 tsp. **Vanilla**

In a saucepan, melt chocolate and margarine and stir. Stir in sugar. Add eggs one at a time, mixing for 2 minutes after each addition. Add flour, vanilla and nuts. Mix well. Pour into 9 x 13 baking pan. Bake for 30–35 minutes in a 350 degree oven.

EGG CUSTARD

"This makes its own crust and can be sliced into pie wedges and served quite easily." Mona Lee Brock—Madill

1/2 cup **Flour**
2/3 cup **Sugar**
4 **Eggs**
1 stick **Margarine**
3 cups **Milk**
1 tbsp. **Vanilla**
1/4 tsp. **Nutmeg**

Mix all ingredients in a blender. Pour mixture into a greased pie plate. Bake at 350 degrees for about 30 minutes.

CARAMEL DUMPLINGS

"I came across this recipe about 30 years ago. My family loved it and I served it many times for special occasions. A scoop of ice cream on top makes it extra special!"
Kathie Stocksen—Enid

1 1/4 cups **Flour**
1 1/2 tsp. **Baking Powder**
1/2 cup **Sugar**
Pinch of **Salt**
2 tbsp. **Butter**
1 tsp. **Vanilla**
1/3 cup **Milk**

Mix dry ingredients together. Cut in butter; add vanilla and milk. Mix and then drop by spoonsful into hot **Caramel Sauce**. Cover tightly and boil over low fire for 20 minutes. (Do not remove cover during boiling time.)
Serves 6.

CARAMEL SAUCE

2 tbsp. **Butter**
1 1/2 cups **Brown Sugar**
1 1/2 cup **Boiling Water**
Pinch of **Salt**

Combine ingredients in large saucepan and boil for 5 minutes.

McClellan—Kerr Arkansas River Navigation System (MKARNS)
From the Port of Catoosa (north of Tulsa), this man-made channel allows freight and grain barges to carry freight 445 river miles to the Mississippi River, a trip of 5 days for a commercial towboat and its barges. The system has 17 locks and dams. The Jean-Pierre Chouteau Hiking Trail, which follows the system from near Ft. Gibson is 60 miles long, has a total of 15 bridges and is on the National Register of Trails

---

CHOCOLATE PIE

"This makes a delicious chocolaty pie. This recipe was given to my by a dear friend, Mary Frech, from our church." Alberta Leierer–Ringwood

1 1/2 cup **Milk**
2/3 cup **Sugar**
3 tbsp. **Cornstarch**
1/4 tsp. **Salt**
4 **Egg Yolks,** slightly beaten

1 tbsp. **Butter**
1 tbsp. **Vanilla**
1 pkg. (12 oz.) **Chocolate Chips**
1 baked (9–inch) **Pie Shell**

Combine milk, sugar, cornstarch and salt in a microwave bowl; beat with whisk or rotary beater until smooth. Microwave on high for 4 minutes. Beat well and continue cooking on high for 1 minute or until thickened; beat well. Beat eggs and a small amount of the hot milk mixture in a small bowl. Add back to milk mixture and beat well. Microwave for 1 1/2 to 2 minutes on ROAST (about 60–70 percent) or until thickened. Stir in butter, vanilla and chocolate until chips are completely melted. Let cool slightly, then pour into pie shell.

POERTZELKI (New Year's Cookies)

"On New Year's Day while we were waiting for the football bowl games to begin on television, Dad would mix up a batch of these cookies."
Henry Ediger–Enid

3 cups **Lukewarm Milk**
4 cups **Flour**
3 cups **Raisins**
1 tbsp. **Salt**
1 tbsp. **Sugar**

6 **Eggs**
2 cakes **Dry Yeast**
Pinch of **Nutmeg**
1 cup **Sugar**

Combine all ingredients except 1 cup sugar. Let mixture rise for 2 hours in a warm place. Drop by teaspoonsful into hot oil and cook until golden brown on both sides. Put 1 cup sugar in a paper bag. Remove cookies from the oil, place them in the bag and shake to coat all sides.

SPUDNUTS
Patsy Warman—Dewey

2 cups **Milk**
1/2 cup **Shortening**
1/2 cup **Sugar**
1 pkg. **Yeast**
1/2 cup warm **Potato Water**
1/2 tsp. **Baking Soda**

1/2 tsp. **Baking Powder**
1/2 tsp. **Nutmeg**
2 **Eggs**, well beaten
1/2 cup **Mashed Potatoes**
Salt to taste
Flour

In a saucepan, bring milk, shortening and sugar to a boil, remove from stove and allow to cool. Mix yeast with potato water and allow to dissolve. Combine baking soda, baking powder, nutmeg and yeast mixture together. Let rise until foamy (about 30 minutes). Add eggs, mashed potatoes, salt and enough flour to make a dough. Place in a warm area and allow to rise until double in bulk. Roll out, cut into doughnuts, let rise again. Deep fry doughnuts until golden brown. Glaze with **Powdered Sugar Glaze.**

POWDERED SUGAR GLAZE

1/2 cup **Water**
1 tsp. **Vanilla**
1/4 stick **Butter**
1 lb. **Powdered Sugar**

Boil water, vanilla and butter together. Add powdered sugar and bring back to a boil for 1 minute.

Fort Sill Military Reservation and National Historic Landmark
Just 5 miles north of Lawton, Fort Sill is headquarters of the U.S. Army Field Artillery. The Old Post Area, retaining its frontier atmosphere, is where the graves of Geronimo and other famous American Indians can be found. Fort Sill museum preserves the history of the American Indian Territory and of U.S. field artillery. Missile Park contains U.S. Army missiles and rockets that date from 1944 to the present, including a display about Desert Storm artillery.

CHOCOLATE CHIP COOKIES

"Making cookies was a favorite pastime when we were growing up. This is my mom's recipe and I think it's the best cookie ever."
Joyce Yauk—Enid

1 cup **Crisco®**
1 cup **Brown Sugar**
1/2 cup **Sugar**
1 tsp. **Vanilla**
2 **Eggs**

2 1/4 cups **Flour**
1 tsp. **Baking Soda**
1 tsp. **Salt**
1 cup chopped **Nuts**
1 pkg. (11.5 oz.) **Milk Chocolate Chips**

Cream shortening, sugars and vanilla until light and fluffy; add eggs and beat well. Combine flour, baking soda and salt, stir into creamed mixture a little at a time. Stir in nuts and chocolate chips. Drop by teaspoonsful onto cookie sheet; bake in a 375 degree oven for 8—10 minutes.
Makes about 5 dozen cookies.

ICE BOX COOKIES

"We always make these cookies during the Thanksgiving and Christmas holidays." Donna Lamb—Drummond

2 cups **Brown Sugar**
1 cup **Margarine**
2 **Eggs**
4 cups **Flour**
1 tsp. **Baking Soda**

1 tsp. **Cream of Tartar**
1 tsp. **Cinnamon**
1/2 tsp. **Salt**
1 cup chopped **Walnuts**

Cream sugar and margarine. Add eggs. Combine dry ingredients and sift into sugar mixture; stir well. Add walnuts and stir well. Shape into a roll that is 2 inches in diameter and wrap in foil. Store in refrigerator overnight. Slice roll into 1/4—inch thick cookies and bake in 350 degree oven until light brown.

SMAZENKY (Filled Doughnuts)
"This recipe was passed down to me by my husband's grandmother and her family who are Czechoslovakian descent."
Martha Gabriel-Hennessey

1 pkg. **Yeast**	1 **Egg Yolk**
1/4 cup **Warm Water**	1 1/2 tsp. **Salt**
1 1/2 cups **Lukewarm Milk**	2 tbsp. **Sugar**
1/4 cup **Wesson® Oil**	4 cups **Flour**
1 **Egg**	

Dissolve yeast in warm water. Combine with the next 6 ingredients and 2 cups flour. Beat well. Add remaining flour and combine. Let rise until doubled. Flatten dough on a floured surface to about 1/2-inch thick. Cut circles with biscuit cutter. Stretch each circle slightly and let rest five minutes. Place one teaspoon **Poppy Seed Filling** on each circle. Moisten edges with water and seal in half-moons. Fry in hot oil until brown. Drain on towels and roll in sugar or other toppings.

POPPY SEED FILLING

1 lb. **Poppy Seeds,** ground
3/4 qt. **Applesauce**
1/2 cup **Milk**
1 can (14 oz.) **Eagle Brand® Sweetened Condensed Milk**
Sugar, to taste

Mix all ingredients together. Cook in a saucepan or in the microwave until thick, stirring often.

Did you know?
Oklahoma has more man-made lakes than any other state, with more than one million surface acres of water and 2,000 more miles of shoreline than the Atlantic and Gulf coasts combined.

BAKLAVA (A Middle Eastern pastry)

"My sister and I have made this pastry for about 20 years. We start during the Thanksgiving holiday season and usually make a dozen batches. We freeze the pastry, give some as Christmas gifts and take some to parties and family gatherings. In 1999, I entered this in the Oklahoma Pecan Food Show and won. Grand Champion." Roberta Morrow–Roff

FILLING:
2 cups **Pecans,** chopped
2/3 cup **Sugar**
1/2 tsp. **Cinnamon**
1/2 tsp. **Orange–Flower Water**
Mix thoroughly, cover with a damp
cloth and set aside.

SYRUP:
1 1/2 cups **Sugar**
3/4 cup **Water**
1 tbsp. **Lemon Juice**
1 cup **Honey**

In a saucepan, combine sugar, water and lemon juice; bring to boil. Reduce heat and simmer 30 minutes. Remove from heat and stir in honey. Set aside to cool.

PASTRY:
1 pkg. (1 lb.) **Phyllo**   1 1/2 lb. **Butter,** softened

Butter an 11 x 16 baking sheet. Line with a layer of phyllo and brush top of phyllo with butter. Continue layering and buttering. On the 8th layer, spread the filling evenly over all. Continue layering and buttering the phyllo until all sheets are used. Cut the pastry into diamond shapes. Bake at 350 degrees for 50–60 minutes or until golden brown. Remove from oven and spoon syrup mixture over all. Let stand several hours or overnight. Transfer pastry to airtight containers and refrigerate or freeze. Thaw pastry in the refrigerator when ready to use. Note: When working with the phyllo, keep all the sheets covered with a towel to keep them from drying out.

GRANDMA FREY'S CHRISTMAS COOKIES

"I can't remember a Christmas that my mother didn't make these cookies for us." Wynona Kuhnemund–Lahoma

1 cup **Butter**
2 cups **Sugar**
2 **Eggs**
1 tsp. **Vanilla**
1 tsp. **Baking Soda**

1/2 tsp. **Baking Powder**
1/2 tsp. **Salt**
5 1/2 cups **Flour**
1/2 cup **Sour Milk**
1/2 cup **Sour Cream**

Cream butter and sugar; add eggs and vanilla and mix well. Sift dry ingredients together and add to butter mixture alternately with sour milk and sour cream. If dough is too hard to handle, cool in refrigerator. Rollout, but not too thin. Cut into various shapes with cookie cutters. Bake on lightly greased cookie sheets at 375 degrees for 8–10 minutes. When cool, frost with **Christmas Cookie Icing.**

CHRISTMAS COOKIE ICING

4 1/2 cups **Powdered Sugar**
1/2 stick **Margarine**

2 tsp. **Vanilla**
4 1/2 tbsp. **Half and Half**

Mix all ingredients together thoroughly.

JIM'S NO—BAKE COOKIES

Jim Hays–Oklahoma City

2 cups **Sugar**
1/2 cup **Milk**
1/4 cup **Cocoa**
1 stick **Butter**

1/2 cup **Peanut Butter***
1 tsp. **Vanilla**
3 cups **Quick Oats**

Combine sugar, milk, cocoa, and butter in large saucepan and bring to boil; boil for 1 minute. Add peanut butter, vanilla and oats. Mix well. Drop mixture, about 1 teaspoon per cookie, onto wax paper. Let stand for several hours. Note: Nuts, coconut or raisins may be added if desired. *Plain or crunchy

MOM'S CHOCOLATE PIE
'My mom is the best pie maker! This is our family's favorite."
Teresa Wuerflein–Kremlin

1 cup **Sugar**	3 **Eggs,** separated
3 tbsp. **Cocoa**	1 tsp. **Vanilla**
1/4 tsp. **Salt**	2 tsp. **Margarine**
1/2 cup **Flour**	1 cooked **Pie Shell**
2 cups **Milk**	

In a saucepan, mix sugar, cocoa, salt and flour. Add 1 1/2 cups milk. Mix together well and cook over medium heat. In a separate bowl, mix egg yolks (reserving whites for Meringue) and the remaining 1/2 cup milk. Add to cocoa mixture just before it starts to boil. Cook until mixture thickens; add vanilla and margarine. Pour into pie shell. Top with Meringue and bake at 400 degrees for 5 minutes.

MERINGUE:

3 **Egg Whites**	1 tsp. **Flour**
2 tbsp. **Sugar**	Few drops of **Vanilla**

Beat egg whites until stiff: blend in sugar, flour and vanilla.

PEANUT BUTTER BARS
Angela D. Hahn–Okeene

1/3 lb. **Graham Crackers**	1 cup softened **Butter** or **Margarine**
1 cup **Peanut Butter**	1 lb. **Chocolate Chips**
1 box (1 lb.) **Powdered Sugar**	

Crush graham crackers to a fine crumb. Add peanut butter, powdered sugar and butter. Mix by hand until mixture is stiff and pulls away from side of bowl. Butter the sides and bottom of a 5 x 8 baking pan. Put mixture in pan and pat down until top is smooth. In a double boiler melt chocolate chips until smooth. Pour over peanut butter mixture and put in refrigerator until set. Cut into bars.

RUTH'S RHUBARB PIE & FOOLPROOF PIE CRUST

"These recipes have been in my family for at least 40 years."
Jeannine R. Bennett—Enid

RUTH'S RHUBARB PIE:
3/4 cup **Sugar**
1/3 cup **Cornstarch**
2 (9-inch) **Foolproof Pie Crusts** (see below)
1 pkg. (16oz.) frozen **Rhubarb**, partially thawed or 2 cups fresh, sliced
2 tbsp. **Butter**
1/2 **Lemon,** juiced
Sugar to taste

Preheat oven to 400 degrees. Stir together sugar and cornstarch. Pour rhubarb into **Foolproof Pie Crust**. Pour sugar mixture over the rhubarb and dot with butter. Sprinkle with lemon juice. Cover with top curst and seal; flute edges. Cut slits into top curst and sprinkle with sugar. Bake 40–45 minutes or until crust is brown and juice begins to bubble through slits in crust.

FOOLPROOF PIE CRUST:
4 cups **Flour**   1 tbsp. **Vinegar**
1 3/4 cups **Shortening**   1 **Egg**
1 tbsp. **Sugar**   1/2 cup **Water**
2 tsp. **Salt**

In a large bowl, mix together the flour, shortening, sugar and salt until crumbly. In another bowl, combine vinegar, egg and water. Combine mixtures and chill for 15 minutes. Divide dough into three pieces. Roll 2 pieces of dough out for top and bottom crusts. Unused dough may be stored in refrigerator for three days or frozen. If frozen, allow to soften at room temperature before using.

Makes 3 (9-inch) pie crusts.

PFEFFERNÜESSE (Peppernuts)

"My great, great grandmother, Trientje Husman Janssen, was born in Stiekelkamperfehn, Ostfriesland in Northwestern Germany. She married George Johnson in the 1880's and moved to Lahoma, Oklahoma around 1902. She passed down her Pfeffernuesse recipe to us. These are nickel-sized hard cookies that are great to dunk in coffee or hot chocolate. We always make them at Christmas." Kris Ediger–Enid

2 cups **Dark Syrup**
2 cups **Shortening**
1 tsp. **Baking Powder**
2 cups **Sugar**
1 cup strong, liquid **Coffee**
1 tsp. **Baking Soda**

1 tsp. **Salt**
1 tbsp. **Pepper**
1 tbsp. **Nutmeg**
1 tbsp. **Ginger**
1 tbsp. **Cloves**
2 tbsp. **Cinnamon**

Mix all ingredients together in a very large bowl. Add enough Flour to make a very stiff dough. Refrigerate for a few hours. Roll out and cut dough into nickel-sized cookies, Bake in a 375 degree oven until brown. Store in large glass jars. The longer they sit, the better the flavor.

MAMA'S PRUNE CAKE

"This is my husband Earl's grandmother's recipe."
Sweet Pea Abernathy–Altus

1 1/2 cup **Sugar**
1 cup **Oil**
1 cup cooked **Prunes**
3 **Eggs**
1 cup **Buttermilk**

2 cups **Flour**
1 tsp. **Baking Soda**
1/4 tsp. **Salt**
1/2 tsp. each: **Nutmeg, Allspice, Cloves**

Place all ingredients in large bowl and mix with mixer. Pour into a tube pan and bake in 350 degree oven for 35 minutes.

QUICK & EASY ICE CREAM

"My mother gave me this recipe about 15 years ago. I use it every chance I get. It is so quick and easy and cleanup is a breeze. The hardest part is waiting for it to get done." Sara Fleming—Covington

2 cans **Sweetened Condensed Milk**
6 cans (12 oz. ea.) **Strawberry—Flavored Soda** (or flavor of your choice)

Pour the sweetened condensed milk in a large mixing bowl. Add three cans of the soda pop. Stir together. Pour this mixture into an ice cream freezer canister. Pour remaining pop into canister and mix together just enough to blend. Freeze according to manufacturer's instructions.

BURNT SUGAR CAKE

"This was one of my mother's favorite cakes."
Mary Beth Lilley—Enid

1 1/2 cup **Sugar**
3/4 cup **Water**
2 **Eggs**
3/4 cup **Shortening**
1 tsp. **Baking Powder**
1 tsp. **Baking Soda**
2 1/2 cups **All—Purpose Flour**
1 cup **Milk**
2 tsp. **Vanilla**

Brown 1/2 cup sugar in a heavy pan until dark brown: pour water over the sugar to make a thick syrup. Set aside to cool. Cream balance of sugar, eggs and shortening well (3 minutes with electric mixer or 4 minutes on rotary beater). Combine baking powder, baking soda and flour and add, alternately with milk, to sugar mixture. Cream well after each addition. Add sugar syrup and mix well. Add vanilla and mix well. Bake in two well-greased and floured 9-inch cake pans in preheated 350 degree oven for 30 minutes. Frost with your favorite frosting while cake is still slightly warm.

LILL'S BLUE RIBBON CHOCOLATE CAKE

"This recipe has won first place the past four years at the Pontotoc County Fair." Lillian Kidwell–Allen

1 cup **Butter**	1/4 tsp. **Salt**
2 1/2 cups **Sugar**	1 cup **Buttermilk**
2 **Eggs**	2 tsp. **Vanilla**
2 1/2 cups **Flour**	2 tsp. **Baking Soda**
6 heaping tbsp. **Cocoa**	1 cup **Boiling Water**
1 tsp. **Cornstarch**	

Cream butter and sugar; beat in eggs. Mix together flour, cocoa, cornstarch and salt. Add to creamed mixture, alternating with buttermilk and beating well between additions. Add vanilla. Dissolve the baking soda in the boiling water and beat into cake mixture. Pour mixture into 3 (8-inch) layer pans and bake at 350 degrees for 20 minutes. Cool on wire rack. Frost with Chocolate Frosting.

CHOCOLATE FROSTING

1 stick softened **Butter**	1 tsp. **Lemon Juice**
5 heaping tbsp. **Cocoa**	1 **Egg**
2 tsp. **Vanilla**	1 box **Powdered Sugar**

Cream butter and cocoa together. Add vanilla, lemon juice, and egg and beat again. Add powdered sugar and blend all together well.

Jasmine Moran Children's Museum In Seminole
This hands-on museum is shaped like a child-size town, complete with street signs, courthouse, grocery store, fire station, hospital and television studio. Children can assume various roles in the community by donning a grocer's apron, dentist's jacket or a firefighter's uniform.

FRUIT COCKTAIL PUDDING CAKE
"This is my mother's recipe. She often made it for special occasions."
Linda Pierce—Enid

2 cups **Flour**
1 1/2 cups **Sugar**
1 tsp. **Salt**
2 tsp. **Baking Soda**
2 **Eggs**

2 tsp. **Vanilla**
1 can (16oz.) **Fruit Cocktail**
1/2 cup **Nuts**
1/4 cup **Brown Sugar**

Combine first six ingredients in an electric mixer bowl and blend together well. Add fruit cocktail, including juice. Stir until evenly mixed. Pour into a greased and floured 9 x 13 baking pan. Sprinkle top with nuts and brown sugar. Bake in a 325 degree oven for 45 minutes. Serve warm, with ice cream or whipped topping.

SHOO—FLY PIE
"This is Pennsylvania—style Shoo Fly Pie without the crust. I use sorghum instead of molasses in my recipe."
Mary Frances Myers—Tulsa

1 cup **Molasses** or **Sorghum**
2 1/2 cups **Boiling Water**
1 tsp. **Baking Soda**
4 cups **Flour**

1 tsp. **Salt**
2 1/4 cups (1 lb.) **Light Brown Sugar**
1 cup **Vegetable Oil**

Combine molasses and boiling water. Combine remaining ingredients with an electric mixer. Reserve 1 cup for topping. Combine the balance of the dry mixture with the molasses. Pour into an 11 x 13 ungreased pan. Sprinkle with reserved topping. Bake in a 350 degree oven for 45 minutes.

INEZ'S OATMEAL CAKE
"This recipe has been used in the Claymore family for over four generations." Inez Claymore–Oklahoma City

1 1/4 cups **Boiling Water**
1 stick **Butter**
1 cup **3 Minute Oats**
1 cup **White Sugar**
1 cup **Brown Sugar**

2 **Eggs**
1 1/2 cup **Flour**
1/2 tsp. **Salt**
1 tsp. **Baking Soda**
1/2 tsp. **Nutmeg**

In large mixing bowl, pour boiling water over butter and oats; mix and let stand for 20 minutes. In a small bowl, combine both sugars and the eggs. Stir into butter mixture. In another small bowl, combine the flour, salt, baking soda and nutmeg. Combine the flour mixture with the butter mixture. Grease a 9 x 13 baking pan. Pour in cake batter. Bake in a preheated 350 degree oven until cake springs back or toothpick inserted into center comes out clean. Pour hot **Coconut–Pecan Icing** onto middle of cake and spread to edges. Place cake under broiler (4–5 inches from element) and broil until golden brown.

COCONUT—PECAN ICING

1 stick softened **Butter**
1/4 cup **Milk**
1/2 cup **White Sugar**

1/2 tsp. **Vanilla**
1 cup chopped **Pecans**
1 cup shredded **Coconut**

Mix all ingredients together in a non–stick coated skillet. Bring to boil for just a few seconds.

LEMON CHIFFON PIE
Angela D. Hahn–Okeene

1 can (12 oz.) frozen **Lemonade**
1 can (14 oz.) **Sweetened Condensed Milk**

1 sm. container **Cool Whip®**
2 (8") **Graham Cracker Pie Crusts**

Combine first three ingredients; beat until frothy. Pour into pie crusts. Freeze; serve frozen.

CANDY CANE COFFEE CAKE

This original recipe won champion/sweet bread category in the Oklahoma Wheatheart Contest at the Oklahoma State Fair. Lenne Hutchison–Canton Courtesy of Oklahoma Wheat Commission, Oklahoma City

1 cup **Warm Water**
2 cups **Sour Cream**, at room temperature
3 tbsp. **Yeast**
1 cup **Sugar**
1 1/2 tsp. **Salt**
1 **Egg,** room temperature
1/2 cup melted **Shortening**, cooled to lukewarm temperature
6–7 cups **Bread Flour**
Butter, melted

APRICOT FILLING:

1 oz. toasted **Almonds**   18 oz. **Apricot Preserves**
1 oz. toasted **Walnuts**   1/4 cup chopped **Maraschino Cherries**

ICING:

2 cups **Confectioners Sugar**
2 tbsp. **Water**
1 tsp. **Vanilla**

In a large bowl, combine warm water, sour cream, yeast and sugar; let stand until doubled. Add salt, egg and shortening and enough flour to make a thick batter. Blend until smooth; then add remaining flour, enough to make dough easy to handle. Knead for 8 to 10 minutes. Let rise until doubled. Combine filling ingredients and set aside. Punch down and divide dough into thirds. Roll each section of dough to 15 x 6-inch rectangles. Place on greased cookie sheets. With scissors , make 2-inch deep cuts at 1/2-inch intervals on the long sides of the rectangle. Spread one-third of the filling down the remaining 2-inch center of each rectangle. Crisscross strips over filling. Stretch dough to 22 inches. Curve to form candy cane. Let rise again until doubled. Bake at 375 degrees for 18–20 minutes. While warm, brush with butter and drizzle canes with icing. Makes 3 candy cane cakes.

TURNER FALLS INN SHEATH CAKE
Paula Williams—Turner Falls Inn, Davis

2 cups **Sugar**
2 cups **Flour**
4 tbsp. **Cocoa**
1 stick **Margarine**
1 cup **Water**
1/2 cup **Crisco®**

1/2 cup **Buttermilk**
2 **Eggs,** beaten
1 tsp. **Baking Soda**
1 tsp. **Cinnamon**
1 tsp. **Vanilla**

Preheat oven to 400 degrees. Combine sugar, flour and cocoa in a large mixing bowl. Place margarine, water and Crisco® in a saucepan. Bring to a rapid boil; pour over sugar and flour mixture; stir well. Add remaining ingredients and mix well. Pour into a greased 16 x 11 baking pan. Bake for 20 minutes. Remove cake from oven and, while still warm, ice with **Powdered Sugar Icing**.

POWDERED SUGAR ICING

1 stick **Margarine**
4 tbsp. **Cocoa**
6 tbsp. **Milk**

1 lb. **Powdered Sugar**
1 tsp. **Vanilla**
1 cup chopped **Pecans**

Combine margarine, cocoa and milk in a saucepan. Heat well. Add remaining ingredients. Beat well; let stand 5 minutes before frosting cake.

Turner Falls
U.S. Hwy. 77 take travelers into the Arbuckle Mountains and Oklahoma's best-known swimming hole, Turner Falls, near Davis. In addition to splashing in a pool fed by a 77-foot waterfall, visitors can explore a wild cave, hike, picnic or camp at the park.

APRICOT DESSERT

"I entertain often. Everyone enjoys this rich dessert handed down from my mother." Andrea Hutchison—Canton

1/2 cup **Butter**
1 cup **Powdered Sugar**
2 **Eggs,** beaten
6 1/2 cups crumbled **Vanilla Wafers**
2 cups drained and chopped **Apricots**
2 cups whipped **Heavy Cream**
1 cup chopped **Pecans**

Melt butter in double boiler; add sugar and eggs; blend. Cook over boiling water for 4 minutes until thick. Pack one-half of the wafer crumbs in bottom of jellyroll pan. Spread the crumbs with the cooked filling which has been cooled; spread half the apricots, half of the nuts; then half of the whipped cream over top of filling. Repeat, starting with the apricots and ending with whipped cream. Top with a sprinkling of additional nuts and remaining wafer crumbs. Chill 24 hours. Serves 16–20.

CHERRY ANGEL FOOD CAKE

**"This recipe was received from a co-worker. It's a hit wherever I take it, as well as at home. Just be sure a one-step mix is used and no other liquid is added. Other fruit pie filling mixes work well, also."
Karen Barnes—Ames**

1-Step Angel **Food Cake Mix**
1 can (20oz.) prepared **Cherry Pie Filling Mix**

Add pie filling mix to dry angel food cake mix. Beat until peaks are formed. Pour into angel food cake pan and bake at 350 degrees for 1 hour. Caution: Do not under-bake. Turn upside down over a pop bottle to cool.

MARY BETH LILLEY

Mary Beth Lilley was born and raised on a Kansas farm. A newspaper reporter and photographer since 1955, she worked on three daily newspapers in Kansas, moving to Oklahoma in 1973. For nearly 23 years she wrote for the Enid News & Eagle. She has published two books featuring popular articles from her weekly column, "From The Lilley Pad." She also wrote a cooking column featuring down-home cooking. Currently she writes a column, "Lines From The Lilley Pad" for The Covington Record, a weekly newspaper in eastern Garfield County. Lilley lives with two indoor cats, Razzy and Tiger Lilley, along with five or more outdoor cats.

RECIPE

Recipe: _____

From: _____

Ingredients: _____ _____

_____ _____

_____ _____

_____ _____

_____ _____

Directions: _____

_____

_____

_____

_____

_____

RECIPE

Recipe: _____

From: _____

Ingredients: _____ _____

_____ _____

_____ _____

_____ _____

_____ _____

Directions: _____

_____

_____

_____

_____

_____

If you love cookbooks, then you'll love these too!

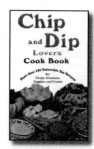

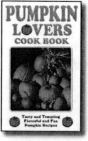

QTY	TITLE	PRICE	TOTAL
	Burrito Lovers' Cook Book	9.95	
	Chili Lovers' Cook Book	9.95	
	Chip & Dip Lovers' Cook Book	9.95	
	Citrus Lovers' Cook Book	9.95	
	Easy BBQ Recipes	9.95	
	Easy BBQ Sauces	9.95	
	Grand Canyon Cook Book	9.95	
	Low Fat Mexican Recipes	9.95	
	New Mexico Cook Book	9.95	
	Mexican Family Favorites Cook Book	9.95	
	Quick-n-Easy Mexican Recipes	9.95	
	Salsa Lovers' Cook Book	9.95	
	Sedona Cook Book	9.95	
	Tequila Cook Book	9.95	
	Texas Cook Book	9.95	
	Tortilla Lovers' Cook Book	9.95	
	Veggie Lovers' Cook Book	9.95	
	Western Breakfast	9.95	

US Shipping & Handling Add	1-3 Books: 5.00	
[for non-domestic ship rates, please call]	4-9 Books: 7.00	
	9+ Books: 7.00 + 0.25 per book	
	AZ residents add 8.1% sales tax	
	(US funds only) Total:	

Please make checks payable to:
Golden West Publishers
4113 N. Longview,
Phoenix, AZ 85014

☐ Check or money order enclosed
☐ MC ☐ VISA ☐ Discover ☐ American Express Verification Code:_____

Card Number:_____ Exp._____

Signature: _____

Name_____Phone: _____

Address _____

City_____State_____ZIP _____

Email _____

Prices are subject to change.

Visit our website or call us toll free for a free catalog of all our titles!